SPICY NATURAL REMEDIES

SPICY NATURAL REMEDIES

How I Survived Cancer, and Other Illnesses,

with Using Positive Thinking

and Natural Remedies

By

Virginia Sullinger King

This book is dedicated to my children. My love for them and the determination to be there for them as they needed me was what led me to hang on to life and to want to stay strong in faith believing that God would save me. I wrote this book so that anyone who may be interested in knowing how I survived cancer and other illnesses for so long may be encouraged to find a reason to fight for their life and to have faith until the end that we have a higher power above us, and to love every day we are given. Also, it is in memory of my mother who died too soon, my sisters who died and survived, my grandmother who had cancer for over fifteen years who taught me about natural remedies, my half-sister and cousins who died of cancer, and my ex-mother-in-law whom I totally adored who also died of cancer. And it is in remembrance of my father who worked hard for us when I was a child, my brothers who left this world behind them, my grandfather who was as rough as a grizzly bear but soft hearted as a teddy bear, and of my uncle who taught me about the love and power of God.

CONTENTS

PREFACE

Spicy Natural Remedies is a true story about how I survived cancer, and other illnesses, with using positive thinking and natural remedies. They gave up on me, but I didn't give up on myself. I used natural remedies that I had learned about from my grandmother, and by staying positive that everything was going to be okay by my uncle. I tell a little about my background, and how I learned about natural remedies, the power of God and positive thinking, and I share some of my struggles from being too sick to care for myself. I tell about problems with some relationships due to cancer causing my loved ones to back away from me, the process I went through having a double mastectomy, and being prepared for breast implants after having the mastectomy. I describe foods I ate to help with inflammation and other symptoms I was having, and the physical exercises I done to help with vertigo, and my meditation method to focus on positive thinking and training my body to fight cancer to build my energy and to have a better quality of life.

Names and places may have been changed so as
to protect innocent people's privacy.

CHAPTER ONE

Learning About God and
Natural Remedies

I WIN

I Am A Cancer Survivor

How Do I Say Those Words Out Loud with So Many People Hurting? I asked myself that question before trying to write about what God has done for me with my surviving the horrible things I have been through. Hello, my name is Virginia. I am grateful to say that among other things I have survived I am also a cancer survivor. According to some doctors that I met I should have been dead several times over. I have a rare enzyme deficiency disease that keeps me from being able to use, or eat, most products that are available to us in the average store. I am also limited to what medications I can have because a lot of things work the opposite on me and because of my allergies. That has created a serious problem several times in my life. Especially when I was diagnosed with having Invasive Ductal Carcinoma breast cancer.

I feel that I was blessed to have grandparents who still used old fashioned home remedies, and who took the time to teach me some of them when I was a child. Those old fashioned remedies later helped me to survive cancer and other medical issues that I have had when I could not take other medication, and helped me with some side effects that were making my system weak. My mother's mother was a cancer survivor too. However, she didn't have breast cancer, instead she had Lymphoma Cancer, and she used her own remedies to help her live for many years with cancer. It wasn't even cancer that took her out. It was a blood clot from getting a staph infection from someone caring for someone else that had staph. My sister, and a couple of uncles, had liver cancer. I have lost my first-born son and a couple of grandchildren from being born premature, cousins to ovarian cancer, my half-sister and a couple of cousins to breast cancer.

I lost my father, my eldest brother, and a couple of uncles to Leukemia complications and Lupus. They are all gone. So is my momma. I miss them all very much. I felt guilty when my sister died after I had survived the things that I had been through. I couldn't understand why God let me live and not them. Not some friends of mine, or the babies who died next to my youngest daughter who was born with a major heart condition. What made me so special? I don't know. Maybe it was to live so that I could tell you what I lived and survived through. Maybe it was just because it wasn't my time yet. All I know is that I was so sick that I was slowly dying. I couldn't work from being so sick, and later I became homeless because I had no relatives that lived close to me, and no one in my family knew I was as sick as I was because I was too sick to know how sick I was.

MY BACKGROUND

My family background was full of variety. I was born in St. Louis Missouri, but I was raised in Arizona, Arkansas, Illinois, Iowa, and Florida with my moving back to Missouri several times. I attended Social Work classes at a University in Arkansas with Freshman Honors. When I was a child my family was half Pentecostal, half Baptist, and mixed with different nationalities. My father was a hard core veteran paratrooper who worked hard as a diesel mechanic. He believed that everyone should work for what they got, and that everyone had a right to defend themselves, and they had the responsibility to defend those who could not defend themselves. My father also believed in giving you a good old-fashioned spanking if you got out of line. He, like his father, loved antiques and buying older houses. He would buy old fixer uppers and then renovate them. He would sell them after we lived in them for at least six months, and then he would take the money he received from that house to buy another house and do it again.

Dad taught me how to work on those old houses and when we were done with them, they looked almost new. Dad ran our house like we lived on a military base. In bed early, up early, and chores had to be done before anything else could be done. My daily chore was laundry. I remember hanging clothes up and taking them down off of the clothes lines he had put up in our back yard. No matter what the temperature was like, I was out there taking clothes down, folding them, and putting them in a big white clothes basket. I remember a few times it was so cold that the clothes were frozen solid on the clothesline. Mom and I had to hang them up inside the house on clothes hangers. Those clothes were hanging all over the house on the door facings and looked funny hanging straight out like a board. I remember one day when I watched a shirt thaw out, and how it slowly relaxed and laid down the way it should have been laying if it had not been frozen. After gathering the laundry, I had to iron everything with sprinkles of water and spray starch. Everything except Dad's underwear. He wanted them ironed too, but not with starch.

My mother was a Certified Public Accountant who also enjoyed being a homemaker. She used her mother's natural remedies on us when we were sick. My mother was very quiet and well mannered. Not real prissy, but very lady like. I truly loved watching my mother eat at the table. She was so delicate. Not stiff or ridged like a lot of stuck up people are. Instead, she was just comfortable being herself and with having table manners. I remember that she sat with her hands folded when watching television, or when visiting somewhere. She loved to read, bake, and make dresses for us girls. I guess I turned out to be a mixture of them both. I was a girly tom-boy, because by the time I was thirteen years old I could climb trees, play basketball and baseball, fight like a man, rebuild a carburetor, drive a three speed truck, and help work on houses. I could lay shingles, pop the ridge, lay trim work, and help paint those old houses dad bought to fix up and resell. I also loved what some people would call domestic stuff like sewing, painting, writing, playing a French Horn, and learning proper table etiquette.

My mother never done the discipline in our home. She would always leave that to my father. If absolutely needed she would throw out a statement that if we didn't do like we were told to do, she would tell my father when he got home. That was usually enough to get everyone on the same page real fast. She knew dad was tough on us for our own good, but she also knew that we needed a little freedom too. On Saturdays after my chores were done, mom would let me watch the music shows on television before dad got in from work. I loved to dress up in my high heels and sizzlers, and then I would practice dancing just so I could display my new move at the community dance that night if my sister and I were allowed to go. It was the highlight of the week. That is, unless I was able to go to St. Louis or West Memphis for the weekend or summer.

In St. Louis, I loved visiting my grandparents on both sides. On my dad's side his stepmother was like my mother. Very feminine, and a true holy roller Pentecostal if there ever was one. Dad's dad was Pentecostal too, only he had some rough edges on him. He stood a little over seven-foot-tall and was almost as round as I was tall. He owned several city blocks with an antique store on South Broadway, and over one hundred rent houses and apartments. No one would have ever believed that after my dad's natural mother died my grandfather spent time in prison for moonshining when my dad was just a child. My father, and his brothers, had to go live with their grandparents and aunt until he was released. Later, after he got out of prison, he done odd and end work to support himself.

When I was younger, he would tell us about his bear wrestling days. That's right. He wrestled bears! He told us that on Saturdays he would wrestle bears whose claws had been pulled out, and if he could stay in the ring long enough he would get fifty dollars. Every story he had was about a different bear, and he would have everyone in suspense describing how the bears would slap him around. He told us about how a couple of them tried to sit on him. But since he was a pretty good size man, with muscles almost as big as his belly, they met their match. He would box them around like rubber balls. I thought he was just telling big whoppers, but as it turned out he really did wrestle bears for fifty dollars. One day after he got done telling one of his stories, I told him a story of my own. I told him about how a big rat would come into my bedroom at night and sit on the end of my bed. And how the rat told me that if I didn't go tell my mamma that he wanted some bacon he was going to eat my toes off. Everyone got quiet. Then they suddenly burst out laughing!

Grandpa jumped up out of his old chair and picked me up and swung me around calling me his little Windy. From that day forward I was known as "Wendy" on both sides of the family. For years my grandfather woud brag to his friends about his little story teller. As I got older, I was able to hang around the antique store more. He told me about how he got started in antiques. He had bought an old lamp and table at an auction one day, and later some antique dealer offered him a lot of money for them. He figured there must be money in the old stuff people got rid of. So, he started buying and reselling old stuff until one day he could buy the building he had opened his store in. It was U shaped and three stories tall with apartments on the second and third floors. The rent he got from his tenets, and the antiques he sold, was how he was able to build his little empire. I loved those antiques and hanging out in the store. I would take my time looking at the details on all of the beautiful old furniture and paintings and learned how to play on the old organs and pianos.

I can still remember the different smells from the different types of wood and cloth. For my tenth birthday my grandfather gave me a wooden antique jewelry box that use to set on a shelf high above everything else. Many times, my dad and my uncles offered to buy it from my grandfather. They used to argue over who was going to buy it and they would try to outbid each other. Grandpa always told them, and anyone else who tried to buy it, that he was saving it for someone special. Their mouths dropped like they had cement in them when they watched him give it to me for my birthday. It was over two hundred years old, and it looked like a miniature dresser that had two sets of drawers on each side with a picture box in the middle. In the picture box, it had a picture of Jesus hanging on a cross in the background with a slim trim of what looked like gold that lined the edge of the picture. Also, in the box was what looked like dried bushes in the bottom corners.

He also gave me an antique dresser that looked just like the miniature jewelry box. Only it didn't have a picture box in the middle. Instead, it had a beautiful wooden table with a round mirror on the back of it. I cherished that jewelry box, and the dresser. It made me smile every time I looked at it because it reminded me of the tears in Grandpa's eyes when he seen how happy it made me. Years later, after my eldest daughter was born, it was stolen and put up for sale in a country auction for only five dollars, along with almost everything else that I owned. By the time I found out where my stuff had been taken it was too late for me to get it back. I can't begin to tell you how heartbroken I was. I still try to find my treasured jewelry box when I go to flea markets and antique stores. Maybe one day I will get to see it again.

LEARNING ABOUT LIFE

When in St. Louis if I wasn't with my dad's dad and his stepmother, I was with my mom's mother and her stepfather. It was almost like daylight and dark. My Grandma D had twelve children ranging from older than my mother to a year and a half younger than I was. As a matter of fact, Grandma was pregnant with my favorite uncle at the same time my mother was pregnant with me. We grew up like brother and sister. All of my Grandmother's younger children were like my brothers, and my youngest aunt was like an older sister. She was only nine years older than I was, and she would babysit us for Mom and Dad. She was fun to hang out with, and she loved to wash my long blonde hair in the kitchen sink and then braid it. My mom's mother was tough. She was strict because she had to be. Between all of her children and her grandchildren her home always looked like a school that was let out for recess.

My grandmother carried around a switch, and sometimes a miniature baseball bat, and she had no reserves about swinging either one of them at someone if a fight broke out. A couple of my younger uncles would tease her and take off running thinking she couldn't catch them. Wrong! She was fast on her feet, and they learned that she wasn't as old as they thought she was. Grandma was tough, but she had a heart of gold, and always had a way to make things seem better. She was more like my best friend instead of like your average grandmother. She would talk to me about everything you could think of, and she made me feel like I could talk to her about anything at all. If I was upset about something, she used to say things to me like, "It's just temporary Wendy. This too shall pass. Tomorrow will be a new day". She would tell me about something similar that she went through and how she dealt with it. Or, she would tell me of how she handled it wrong, and what she thought she could have done to make it better. It helped me to see things from different viewpoints, and to realize that there were different ways to handle problems.

Grandma would also tell me about old fashioned remedies for just about everything someone could come down sick with. If someone did get sick, both men and women would call her to get advice about what natural remedies they could use to help with whatever was going on at the time. She kept a lot of old traditions alive by keeping different remedies written down in a big receipt box that she kept on her kitchen counter, and she would offer to share them when people asked for help. She was also known for being a good cook. When we moved to Arkansas, she leased a restaurant on the Missouri Arkansas boarder, and people would drive for miles around just to eat her homemade cooking. Especially her homemade biscuits with chocolate gravy at breakfast time. Her mouthwatering lemon meringue pie she fixed fresh every day for dinner was a big hit too. In the summers when I wasn't learning about natural remedies from her, I was learning about God from my Uncle in West Memphis.

Nearly every summer I spent several weeks with my Aunt and Uncle who lived in West Memphis. They too were Pentecostal to the bone. My Uncle, who later died from Lupus and Leukemia complications, was a World War II Army Veteran and member of several Veterans organizations. I always knew that he was active in his community, but it wasn't until I read his Obituary that I found out that he was a member of four brotherhood programs. I also found out that he was in a long list of "Knights" that had extended back to our Scottish roots. He had spent his life helping others and protecting God's people. That was no surprise to me because he always seemed to be a just man, and I never knew of him to turn anyone down for help that he was able to help. I never heard any hateful remarks come out of his mouth about anyone, and he never treated people with addictions, or who was homeless, any less than he treated anyone else. It was because of his teaching me about having faith, and about God's love and power that I was able to fight for my life.

TIMELINE

As I looked back to 1995 when I lived in Northeast Arkansas, I met a doctor who cared enough about his patients to be honest with them about their condition in spite of what insurance companies told him he could and could not say to patients about their medical conditions. My friend recommended him to me after I had made an unhappy trip to see a doctor who told me that the only thing wrong with me was that I needed a man to take care of me. I had been staying sick from fatigue, nausea, headache, anxiety, pain all over my body, and I always kept a rash. I had been to several doctors who could not find out what was wrong with me. That day the doctor told me that all I needed was a man to take care of me! That's right. It cost thousands of dollars for me to hear that. All I could say in response to that was, "You dirty old goat!" I left the room and immediately went to the counter and demanded to speak with the supervisor in charge.

When the supervising doctor arrived, I told him what the other doctor had said to me. Well, as it turned out when an adult goes a long time without having sexual release it causes hormone buildup that actually could cause stress and anxiety. I had to accept the fact that it could be a possible factor because I had not had sex since my son was a baby. He was about seven years old at that time. However, I refused to believe that it was the only reason causing my problems. It just didn't make since to me that a lack of sex would cause so much trouble. If that was the case, I believe that I would have heard something in the news about Nuns and Monks going crazy over not having sex. When I told my friend what he said and what happened afterwards she too could not believe that lack of sex was the only thing causing my problems. She told me to stop wasting my time on that clinic, and to go see her doctor.

I took her advice and made an appointment to see him the next week. While waiting in his waiting room I was amazed by an article I read in a magazine. The cover story was about a woman who stayed sick from something the doctors couldn't identify. As I read the story, I knew that I was in the right place at the right time. The woman in the story had the exact same symptoms that I had been having, and she went through the same thing I had been going through with different doctors telling her there was nothing wrong with her. As it turned out she was sick from allergies. When I went in the back to see the doctor, I took the magazine with me. When he entered the room, he had a nice approachable smile and seemed to have a pleasant personality. He introduced himself to me and asked how he could help me. He sat quietly across from me as I briefly told him about the symptoms I had been having and how I had gone to different doctors who all agreed that there was nothing wrong with me except that I had anxiety.

I told him about how one doctor suspected that I was having anxiety because of stress built up from not having sex for several years. Then I quickly added that I needed a second opinion, and that I was wondering if it was possible to find out if I had the same condition as the woman I read about in the magazine article who had been having the same symptoms that I had been having. Then I held out the book and asked, "Could this be me?" He took the book from me and looked at the page I had it opened to. He asked where I got it from, and I told him that it was in his waiting room. He sat there and took the time to read the article. He laid it down on the counter and said, "I don't know, but we're going to find out."

He told me he was going to send me to see an Ear, Nose, and Throat specialist to have allergy test done on me. Within a few days I was at the other doctor's office being prepped for allergy test. They gave me a shot in one arm to make sure that I wasn't allergic to what the allergy samples were based in, and to a histamine.

Instantly my arm started swelling up like an elephant's leg. It hurt so bad that it felt like it would burst. I started wheezing, my head hurt, I felt weird, I started having anxiety, and got whelps all over my body. The Ear, Nose, and Throat doctor immediately checked me to make sure I was going to be okay, and they gave me a shot to help me with the symptoms I was having, and told me they couldn't finish the test because I was allergic to the sample base. Everything they were going to test me for was based in glycerin. Then they let me sit in a room for over an hour before releasing me. Before letting me go the doctor checked on me again and told me that I was the first patient that he had ever had that was allergic to glycerin. He said our bodies make it, and that it is in almost everything, and that it would definitely be a reason for me to have the symptoms that I had been having. He also told me that there were only a few people in the United States who were known to have an allergy to glycerin.

He said to me that since our bodies make glycerin he couldn't say positively that it was a true allergy, but he was certain that my body wasn't processing it correctly and that because of it my body was over loaded with it and was reacting to the overload by trying to get rid of it. He handed me two boxes of medicine for me to take home to use for the swelling and itchy rash and told me that it would go away in a couple of days. He told me to go back to see the doctor who referred me to him to see what was causing it. Then he told me that he was sorry he couldn't do more for me, and gently guided me out of the room towards the exit station as he said, "Good luck, I will be praying for you." I stood outside of his office still not feeling well and decided to take a cab instead of trying to drive. I walked back in and asked them to call a cab for me. As I waited for the cab, all I could think about was how the one doctor thought all I needed was sex. I wondered what he would have had to say if he had been there when my arm swelled up so big it looked and felt like it was going to pop. Not meaning to be disrespectful, but I remember thinking, "I guess lack of sex caused that too."

RARE DISEASE

I went back to the doctor who sent me for allergy testing, and he said that he needed to do more test on me. I had the lab test done and then went back the next week to get the results. He surprised me when he led me to his personal medical library. He told me to have a seat at a large wooden table that looked like it was made of oak. It was a deep rich brown color and it had been polished beautifully. I could see my reflection in it. He came back with four large hardback books, and then gathered six more books and laid them in front of me separately from the other books. He told me that he would be right back, then he left for a few minutes. He came back with pens and pencils, a pad of paper, and several pages that had been copied from a medical dictionary. He said, "Virginia, you have a rare enzyme disease that is causing your body to not process glycerin right. That is why it seems like some things work the opposite on you than they do on some people." Then he said, "I hate to say this, but I don't know of any treatment for it, or of anyone I can send you to for it."

While pointing at the first set of books he laid down he said, "But there is hope. If you want to live you need to look up everything on these papers in these books here, and then cross-reference them in these books." And then he pointed to the second set of books he put in front of me. Then he said, "Then read every label at home and at the stores when you go shopping. Stay away from everything you find in reference to these lists. If you do, and if you stay away from inverted sugar, you might be able to live one to five years." As he walked toward the door, he told me to take my time, and that I was welcome to go back to finish if I needed to. As he opened the door to walk out, he said, "I'm truly sorry, I wish there was more that I could do for you." For a few minutes I sat at that big beautiful table with the books in front of me in sort of a shock mode. My children were too young to lose their momma. They all had medical conditions. Who would take care of them? One to five years wasn't long enough.

I laid my head down on that shiny table and prayed to God to please help me, and to show me what to do. I remembered my Uncle in West Memphis telling me that we all have a little power of God in us from his Holy Ghost, and that if we truly believed in God and his power that we would be given what we need. We just had to be positive in thinking that we had already received it even if we couldn't see it. I had to be truly thankful for something before I received it. I was thankful. I was thankful that the doctor cared enough to find out what was wrong with me, and I knew that God was leading me in the right direction. All I had to do was listen to the message I was given. So, I did. I researched everything I could that was on the lists he gave me. I knew that doctor had done a lot more than the other doctors had done who wouldn't even try to help me, and that by the grace of God that doctor saved my life by taking the time to teach me what to do and what not to do.

The papers he gave me was about glycerin storage diseases, and about different forms of glycerin. When I first started going through those books, I had no idea that there were so many ways you could use glycerin, or of all the chemical names it was listed in. I spent most of that day going through those books. Some were almost too heavy to pick up, and they were full of words I could not even pronounce. I had to use his dictionary to find out what they meant. I wrote down every form of glycerin that I could find. When I left, I took the list with me along with the copied papers he gave me. I still have those print outs that he gave me, and occasionally if I am not sure about something, I pull them out to research rather or not a word I am not sure about is on the list. When I got home, I looked at every label in the place. There was glycerin in everything I used! No wonder I was so sick.

I realized that it was a miracle that I was even alive. I suddenly felt a sense of protection. God had kept me alive even though I was using the very thing that was killing me. I started making everything I could homemade from scratch ingredients, and I read every label I could when I went shopping. One time I made the mistake of assuming that companies use the same ingredients all the time and made myself sick from not reading labels of products I had already read labels on in a previous shopping spree.

I had gotten used to being able to eat it, so I assumed it was ok. Well, that wasn't the case. Companies change their ingredients to fit the consumer trends and cost of making it. So as of today, I still read almost every label I can when I go shopping. I was grateful for those wonderful doctors. With a few prescriptions I was given, and staying away from glycerin and inverted sugar, I felt better within days. Within weeks I felt better than I had ever remembered feeling. Every day I still thank God for those wonderful doctors. Unfortunately, my primary care doctor later took in a partner who elected that they used a different insurance company. For him to get paid, and to keep his license, he had to fallow their rules. They limited his ability to practice medical care like he had always done. He confidentially told me that he was sick that he couldn't tell patients that they have cancer. He said that he had to leave his own practice just to get out of the mess.

He did not think it was right to limit medical care to patients that they thought were a waste of time and money to treat. Not everyone healed the same. I can honestly say that it broke my heart to see him go through that. He started that clinic, and he cared about all the people he took care of. It was sad that he had to walk away from something he built just because he put his trust in the wrong person, and that he was controlled by insurance companies that limited his ability to give proper medical care. He tried to help his practice be more advanced and have updated x-ray machines and testing ability, but what he ended up with was others telling him who he could and could not help. They stepped in and took over, and turned it into a money-making machine instead of the caring medical facility that it had always been.

When he left the clinic he was not allowed to take any of the patients he had treated through that clinic to his new location, so I was left to deal with doctors who thought people who were terminally ill were a waste of energy and money, or I had to find a new doctor. I didn't know where elso to go. So, I stayed at the same clinic for a little whil until I did not receive the normal blood work that my other doctor had tested me for. It was time for a new doctor. However, I did not meet another doctor or nurse again that went out of their way to help their patients until 2004. I did however, meet a couple of doctors who made sure to put me in my place when I tried to replace the wonderful doctor that I had lost.

FACING BREAST CANCER

In 2003 I was told by a doctor, who refused to do a mammogram on me, that I only had six months to a year and a half to live. In front of my teenage daughter who was born with a serious heart condition, and was facing a serious open-heart surgery in the near future to save her life. She was horrified and hyperventilated, and he just walked out of the room like nothing had happened. He behaved like he had the bedside manors of a doorknob. I was so busy trying to calm my daughter down that I didn't have time to ask him any questions about what had made him come to that conclusion. What was causing the problem? I guess he thought I was going to ask him the same thing I asked every time I walked through his doors, so, he kept going. I had asked him every one to two months for over a year for a referral to have a free mammogram done on me by the traveling medical group who had a breast cancer screening bus that came to our area once a month. My left breast was deformed, and they both were lumpy and sore.

He never took the time to examine them. Instead he told me that if it hurt it wasn't cancer. It was Fibrocystic Disease. When I tried to be more demanding, in a polite way, he accused me of being paranoid because my grandmother had cancer. The day he said that to me in front of my daughter was the last time I seen him. He didn't even wish me well. He just walked out of the room without giving me a return appointment. Maybe he didn't know how to show any empathy without it causing stress on him. I don't know. All I know is that he knew of my daughter's medical condition, and he chose to say those words to me in front of her, and then walked out like her hyperventilating was nothing to be concerned about. That really made me mad. I know that doctors, nurses, and other medical professionals have to be able to turn off their emotions so that they don't get too involved with patients and stress over not being able to help everyone; but what he did crossed the line.

He was unlike one of the other doctors I had seen who cared so much about his patients that he hurt for them when things were out of his control. I remembered one day when I was in the emergency room with my baby sister, and I could hear the medical team working on a family who had been in a car accident. One of the people who had been in the accident had alarms ringing and buzzing like different alarm clocks going off at the same time, and people were running in and out of their room. When I realized what was going on, I prayed for God to have mercy on them, and to forgive them of their sins. The doctor and nurses were talking fast, and calling out different things to do, but those alarms did not silence on their own. Later, I went to the restroom, and I could hear a man crying in the stairwell from the hallway. I thought it was a family member of someone in the car accident, so I opened the stairwell door to talk to them and see if I could pray with them and help them find peace.

What I found was a doctor whom I personally knew. This doctor had treated me and my children many times in the emergency room. He was also the doctor who had been working the emergency department that day, and who had been trying to save the person he couldn't save. He was sitting alone on the steps going towards the next flight up, and he was crying like he was truly heartbroken over the situation. I told him that I was sorry he had to go through that, and that it wasn't his fault. I reminded him that when it is our time to go nothing can stop it, and that just because he couldn't save someone who was destined to go, that did not mean he couldn't save someone who was dying to early from something they shouldn't be dying from. Or from being mangled up for the rest of their life from something that hurt them. I also told him that if it wasn't for God using him, and other good doctor's like him, my children would not be alive. He cried even harder with a smile while nodding his head as he let it hang down. I left him alone to pull his self together so that he could help my sister and others in the emergency room.

When he entered my sister's room, I could see that his eyes were still a little red, but he did not have that defeated look in his face like he had earlier in the stairwell. After he treated my sister for nausea, he said thank you to me on his way out of the door. My sister did not like him because he was frank about situations. I loved him because he not only treated symptoms his patients had, he was straight forward about what was causing their symptoms, and because he cared about his patients. He was the opposite of what the doctor was who left my daughter to hyperventilate after telling me I only had about six months to a year and a half to live. Later I found out that the doctor who told me I didn't have cancer was wrong, and that my grandmother, mother, and other older females in my family were right. The lumps and inverted spots in my breast turned out to be cancer symptoms.

It hurt because it was invasive. If it wasn't for the help of a great Nurse Practitioner I had later met, and the awesome doctors that she got me linked up with, life would be a lot darker right now than what it was then. In December of 2004 I was living in Little Rock, and I was working as a machine operator in a factory. The factory closed early one day for inventory, and I decided to go with some other ladies I worked with to the health department to have an annual screening done. It only cost ten dollars to see a nurse and have a breast exam and STD screening. I had not been to a doctor since I was told that I only had six months to a year and a half to live. I figured that if they couldn't do anything for me then going to a different doctor would just be a waste of money that I needed to help me take care of my children. After getting checked into the health department I was taken to an examination room and was able to see a Nurse Practitioner. She literally snapped at me with pure shock when she seen my breast.

She demanded to know why I waited so long to get in there. She asked if anyone had ever told me how to do a self-breast exam like she thought I was too stupid to know how to do one. I explained to her that I had gone to the doctor nearly every month asking for a mammogram. But he told me I was too young to have breast cancer, and that if it hurt it wasn't cancer. I told her that he told me that I was being paranoid because my grandmother had cancer, so I was obsessed with fear of my having it. He had never even looked at my breast or examined them. He just repeated the same thing every time I went in to see him. The only thing he would do for me was tell me that I was dying, and he didn't even say what from, and that I assumed it was from the enzyme disease that I was told I had. She had tears running down her face as she shook her head. She told me not to worry, she was going to get someone who would take care of me.

I had a limited insurance policy that didn't cover breast care, so the Nurse Practitioner called the Department of Health, and she spoke to a lady who was part of a special program for women with breast cancer. Together they arranged for me to have a mammogram done that very same afternoon at a local hospital. After having the test done a very nice and caring Radiologist came in to talk to me. He told me that he needed to do more test on me.

They done a PET Scan on me and drew some blood from me. After that I was led to his office to wait for him. I knew from the nurse's reaction, and the doctor saying that he needed to do more test, that it had to be worse than the doctor I tried to have a mammogram ordered for me said it was. He came in with another doctor, and a nurse, and told me that he was almost certain that

I had breast cancer, but only a biopsy could confirm it. He told me that he had spoken to the caseworker who had referred me to him, and they both agreed that I should have the biopsy done as soon as possible. He told me that he had taken the liberty of calling a friend of his who was one of the best Surgeon Oncologist in the region. They had already set me up an appointment for the next Monday. I told him that I couldn't take off work, and that my insurance wouldn't cover it. He told me it had already been taken care of and not to worry about it. Well, after all that in one day how was I not supposed to worry?

I kept my appointment that next Monday. When the famous doctor walked in the examination room, and introduced himself, I could tell right off that he was very nice. He pulled back the paper gown to examine me, and after examining me he closed it, and sat down on his roller stool. Both my breasts were inverted and had deep dimples in them. Especially the left. He asked me how long I had been that way. I told him for a couple of years, and explained to him about the doctor who refused to examine me because I told him it hurt and about how he thought I was just paranoid because of my grandmother having cancer, and how he said I was just a hypochondriac. He apologized to me in behalf of the other doctor's lack of experience with cancer and told me that he agreed with the Radiologist.

He too was almost certain that I had breast cancer. He told me he needed to do a biopsy, and that he wanted to do it that coming up Wednesday. I wanted to protest, but after almost begging for a mammogram for over a year I didn't dare try to make up any excuses to get out of it. I had repeatedly requested a mammogram, but I guess I never really thought about what would come after having one. I agreed, and then after he gave me a few short instructions about talking to his nurse who would guide me through the setup procedure he smiled and told me not to worry. He told me he would take good care of me, and then he gave me a big strong hug. Not a fake hug or a sexual hug. It was a real hug that said, "I care." I knew that he cared about his patients like the doctor in the stairwell and the doctor I had in 1995. I knew that I could trust him to take good care of me. The surgery was only two days away. I only had two days to arrange for a babysitter for my son, and to arrange transportation to be picked up after having the surgery. I bought the list of things the nurse said I would need after surgery and had pre-surgery blood test drawn.

Later that night I sat on the edge of my bed wondering just how the doctor I had asked repeatedly for a mammogram could be so insensitive and arrogant as to not even want to examine me. Did he really think I didn't have cancer? Or did he think I would die from the enzyme disease before I would from cancer? Either way he wouldn't like it if it happened to him. I wasn't mad though, and for some odd reason I wasn't scared either. I felt relieved because it was confirmation that I wasn't just imagining it like the doctor said I was. I not only needed a mammogram I also needed surgery. Two days later I went into the hospital to have the biopsy done. The outpatient surgery lobby was full of people. I sat for what seemed like hours waiting for my turn to go in the back. I started getting nauseated from being hungry. I had not been able to eat anything since the night before for precautionary reasons for the surgery. They said it was standard, and that I could get sick to my stomach and aspirate fluid back into my lungs. They didn't know that going hungry made me sick to my stomach too. So, either way, as far as my getting sick to my stomach was concerned it did not look good for me.

When they took me in the back room to prep me for surgery, I had a strange since of feeling well. I knew that everything was going to be okay. The nurses were all nice to me, no one looked at me like they thought I was crazy for trying to get rid of what was eating away at my body, nor was anyone talking to me like they thought I was just being paranoid for being able to feel that something was wrong with my body. It wasn't just my body that looked deformed that was the problem, I also hurt in my chest wall all the time. The doctors called it angina, or anxiety. I also had this wierd feeling that my body was sinking, and just wasn't right. The anesthesiologist talked to me and assured me that he would not give me as much anesthesia as I was given in Florida. In our first meeting I had told him about how I had a sinus surgery to remove polyps from my sinus in outpatient surgery in Florida, and the doctors had a hard time trying to wake me up. I also told him that later I had a DNC and freeze treatment to remove abnormal cells from my uterus and cervix, they elected not to give me as much anesthesia for that surgery.

Well, I woke up in the middle of it. They were rushing to put me back out. I still remember waking up and feeling a burning sharp pulling feeling in my stomach, and the doctor yelling at someone. I was put right back out, and then they had a hard time waking me up. At first, I thought I had a bad dream, but then when the doctor apologized to me for it and explained what happened I knew it wasn't a dream. It was an accident, and everything still went as planned and turned out fine. When I told the anesthesiologist about what happened they contacted the hospital in Florida to verify my sensitivity to anesthesia and to find out what type of anesthesia I had problems with. He assured me that they were going to use something different, and that he was going to be right by my side. Then my Surgeon Oncologist visited with me for about thirty seconds to give me a squeeze on my shoulder and to tell me that he would see me in a few minutes.

The next thing I knew I was being given an injection to help me relax, and then I was taken to the surgery room while still in my bed. I remember feeling cold as they turned the corner before going into the surgery room and seeing the ceiling squares as I went by them. Then I seen someone's pretty blue eyes above a white mask who looked down at me and then they gently squeezed my hand. There was soft rock music playing in the background as they rolled me into a small room that had machines in every direction. I remember thinking they liked my kind of music. The Anesthesiologist said something to me and that was the last thing I remember until I woke up in the recovery room. When I started waking up, I could not open my eyes at all.

They felt like they weighed a ton. I could hear people talking in the background, and I could hear machines making beeping noises. My feet felt as heavy as my eyelids did. I couln't move, but I could hear the nurse who was attending to me talking to me and saying my name.

She was telling me that everything went fine, and that I was doing great. I don't remember getting sick, but I do remember being hungry. I was in the recovery room for an hour or so, and then I was released to go home. My doctor was in surgery with another patient of his and could not talk to me at the time. They told me that he would call me within a couple of days to let me know the results. My landlord picked me up from the hospital and took me home. I had no one to stay with me and help me get to the restroom. I was lucky that I slept until my son got a ride home from school I didn't have to wait for a couple of days to get the results. The hugging doctor called me that very night. He told me that I done just fine during the surgery, but he was sorry to tell me that the surgery confirmed what he had suspected. It was malignant, and then he told me that he would know more about it within a few days when he received the Pathology report.

He told me that he would like to see me early the next week and said it would be best if I could take a family member with me to the appointment. Well, that didn't sound to encouraging, but I agreed. I suddenly had a wave of anxiety go over me thinking about my mother-in-law and a few others who died of breast cancer. I guess he could tell, and when he asked if I was okay, I told him I was just having a wave of anxiety. He told me that was normal, and that he would call me in a prescription for it. He told me not to worry and that he would see me in a few days. I sat there a little numb. Not in shock because I had already expected to hear it, but to actually hear it even though in my gut I already knew was on a totally different level. It was no longer a suspicion that had to be explored so that it could be written off as a false alarm. Instead, it was a reality that had to be taken care of as soon as possible. I got my perscription filled befor the pharmacy closed, and then called my grandma and told her she was right. We cried together and then prayed together over the phone.

We both agreed that it felt like it was going to be okay. She told me to go on with my life like nothing had happened, and not to dwell on it because if I dwelled on it I would give cancer control and take me out. I wasn't about to just give up, lay down, and die. Even if I wanted to I didn't even know how to give up. I knew my grandmother was right, and I knew I had to have faith like my uncle told me too. So, I looked at it as just one more thing I could add on to my "been there done that" list. I went to bed that night knowing that all would be fine. I didn't even need the prescription that I had gotten filled. I was fine. When I went to the appointment, I took my friend with me because my family lived several hours away, and they were not able to make it. My friend sat on one end of the coffee table, I sat at the other end of it, and my Surgeon Oncologist sat towards my right at the table. He told us that the area he had biopsied was malignant, and that the cancer was worse than he originally suspected it was. He went on to tell me that it had spread past the biopsy region and that he recommended a mastectomy.

Then he told me that the scans of my right breast looked suspicious too, and that within six months I may have to have the same thing done on the right side. I wasn't worried about losing my breast. I was ready to get the cancer out of me so I could go on with my life and put a check mark next to it on my list of things I needed to do. So, I asked him, "Since you believe that I will have to go through the same thing with the right side later down the road, can you go ahead and remove them both at the same time?" He looked almost excited and said, "Yes I can. I am glad that you asked that, because legally I cannot recommend that to you. I can only do it if the other side looks suspicious too and you request it to be done." He went on to tell me more about the cancer I had while trying to give me hope. He told me that my odds were good because the kind of cancer that I had was slow growing, and that as far as having cancer was concerned, I had the best kind of cancer I could get. He told me that most likely I had it for ten, fifteen, and maybe even close to twenty years. It was so slow growing that it was almost dormant. Once again he apologized to me for the doctor who refused to do a mammogram on me, and told me that with my permission he could send the doctor a copy of my Pathology report so that in the future he wouldn't be so fast to dismiss something without investigating it first. He told me that he didn't normally interfere, but the other doctor needed to know that he was badly mistaken. Then he got real serious looking and told me that by law he had to tell me that if at any time in the future anyone said the word Metastatic to me it meant that cancer had spread to other parts of my body and that it could be terminal. He told me that depending on a person's insurance, and the medical facility they are using, someone with that diagnosis may or may not receive treatment for it.

After that he perked up and said, "But we're not going to be worried about that right now. Right now, we are going to focus on removing the cancer and getting you better." My friend asked if I would be able to get breast implants after I had the surgery. The doctor told him that I was a perfect candidate for immediate reconstruction, and that if I wanted him to, he could give me a referral to see a plastic surgeon. He asked if I had anyone in mind, and I told him no. He told me that there was a plastic surgeon on the same floor and right around the corner from his office. He said that he could send over a referral for me to see him, and that it would make it easier for me having the two offices next to each other. I agreed that I would meet with the Plastic Surgeon. The doctor went on to tell me that he had scheduled the operating room for me for almost two weeks away and told me that his assistant would go over the details with me.

He told me that the Plastic Surgeon's office would be in contact with me to set an appointment with them to make sure that I qualified for implants. Once again, he told me not to worry and that he was going to take care of me. He walked us to the door, gave me a big hug, and told me he would see me soon. His assistant sat down with me and went over the details of what I needed to do to prepare for the surgery. She said that I had to buy sterile wound dressing pads, not eat after midnight the night before, leave my jewelry at home, or have someone to hold it for me, or if I wanted they could have it put in a safe until I went home. I had to take larger than normal tops that opened in the front so as to be able to dress easily and she told me not to be taking aspirin or using lotions with Vitamin E because it thins the blood for at least seven days before surgery. She told me that I would be staying in the hospital for one to four days, and that I needed to get my medication filled the day before the surgery so that I wouldn't have to be concerned about it when I got discharged from the hospital.

Then she gave me my prescriptions to get filled and then filled out a preadmission form for me, and she called the Plastic Surgeon's office next door to see if I could be worked in to see their doctor since I was already there. The doctor had left earlier, but they set me and appointment to see him the next morning. It was set. She was faxing over the referral to the Plastic Surgeon's office, and all I had to do was show up for the surgery and they would take care of everything. I went home, and this time I talked to my mother and my grandmother at the same time on three-way calling. Later that night I told my children, who at that time were 16, 18, and 19 years old. Everyone was calm. That too was set. The next morning, I met the Plastic Surgeon. He reminded me of a boy I had a crush on when I was a teenager. He had a bright smile like a dentist would have, and he looked at me like I looked familiar to him too.

He told me that he had gone over my records, and had spoken to my Surgeon Oncologist, and that he agreed that I would be a good candidate for immediate reconstruction. He told me that he could take my case, but I had to read some literature about breast implants and sign authorization forms before he could operate on me. He said that he would return after I read and agreed to the terms of the surgery. He left the room, and a few minutes later a nurse entered with a hand full of paperwork and pamphlets.

She told me to read everything, and when I was done reading, I could open the door so that she would know I was finished. I read everything, and then she returned and talked to me for a few minutes about the benefits and dangers of having breast implants to make sure that I understood what I was I was getting myself into. After I signed all the paperwork the nurse left the room, and a few minutes later the doctor returned to go over the procedure with me so I would know what to expect during and after surgery.

He told me that he would be in the operating room when I had my mastectomy, and that as soon as my Surgeon Oncologist was finished removing my breast he would step into the other surgeon's place and take over from there. He told me that he would have to slice my chest wall in half one side at a time, like a slab of bacon; then he would place the tissue expanders inside of my chest wall, and close me back up. He said that I would have drain tubes that would have to be emptied several times a day to keep them from getting clogged, and that my wound dressing would have to be changed every day. He told me that I could take a shower, but I had to cover the area with plastic to keep the dressing from getting wet. He also told me that after a couple of weeks my chest should be able to start the expanding process, and that he would inject several "CCs" of fluid into my tissue expanders every one to two weeks to expand them a little more each time.

He said that in the beginning it would be a little uncomfortable, but he would give each procedure time to expand my tissue and relax before injecting more fluid. He told me that as time went on it would be easier as my tissue expanded. He also told me that he wanted to make sure that I understood, because he did not want me to start the procedure and then change my mind later before the process was completed. I told him that I was engaged to be married, that I was sure, and I promised to finish the process. He said, "Great. It's settled then. We will start immediate reconstruction when you have the mastectomy." Afterwards something strange happened. He told me that he needed to take pictures of my breast for before and after pictures and to give him an idea as to how my body is naturally shaped for medical reasons. It felt weird, but I agreed.

On his way out of the examination room he told me to strip everything off and to put on the gown he had laid on the examination table. After he walked out, I took everything off except for my panties. I wrapped the paper gown around me and sat down on the examination table and waited for him to return. When he walked in, he had what looked like a professional camera, and he asked me to stand over to the side of the room in front of him and take off my gown. I did, and he took front and side view pictures of me with my hands to my side and with my hands raised up in the air. Then he told me to turn around so he could take pictures of me from behind. I didn't understand why he wanted pictures of me from the rear and asked him, "why?" He told me that he needed them for comparison pictures in case I have toxicity swelling after having the implants put in. Okay, I could buy that one.

So, I did what I was asked to do. When he was done taking pictures, he told me I could get dressed. As I walked past him towards my clothes, he slapped my butt! Firm! My instinct was to slap his face! I turned toward him, and he told me that I had an abnormally firm backside for someone my age, and he wanted to see if it was naturally that firm, or if it was inflammation. That did not set well with me at all, but I kept my mouth shut. He then walked out of the door telling me he would see me at surgery. I checked out feeling not so sure about that doctor. Maybe he was so comfortable doing that so many times he done it without thinking anything about it, but I think I would have felt more comfortable if he had given me warning that he was going to do it. I'm was sure it wasn't anything sexual, but it defiantly was a surprise I wasn't prepared for, and he was lucky I didn't slap him in the face like I started to. But, I didn't, and life went on like nothing had happened.

BAD INVESTMENT

The appointment with my Surgeon Oncologist set off a chain of events in my personal life. Other than having to deal with breast cancer I also had to deal with the man I was engaged to be married to the next summer, and to whom I had been living with for a year, breaking off our wedding engagement. Three days before my mastectomy he came home and said, "We need to talk." He told me that he cared a lot about me, but he was trying to get to a place in his life where he could be financially set so he could retire early, and that with me he didn't think he could do that. He said, "I'm sorry, but you're a bad investment." I sat there thinking that he was just scared I was going to die. and when I opened my mouth to say that, but he interrupted me by saying that he had rented a truck for my stuff, and that I needed to go stay with my family so that they could take care of me. Then he walked into the kitchen and got some trash bags and went into the bedroom and started taking my things out of the dresser and putting them in a trash bag. I just sat at the kitchen table not wanting to move.

I almost started crying, but if he didn't want to take care of someone who he thought was dying I couldn't force him too. It was my battle. Not his. He loaded my dresser and the extra bed in the spare bedroom into a truck he had rented that was parked outside in our driveway. I had not even realized that he hadn't driven his own truck home until he took my dresser outside to load in the truck. That was when I realized that he had put some thought into what he was doing. He wasn't scared. He just seen me as not being good enough. Like a work horse with bad feet. I started packing my personal things in suitcases and trash bags and helped him load it on the truck. I made sure my breakables and medical belongings were on top and secured, and then I sat on the front steps waiting for him to attach my car to the truck with the car hauler he had rented along with the truck. As I was getting inside the truck he bent down and gave me a kiss on my forehead and handed me fifty dollars rolled up.

He told me the truck was rented for two days, and that once I got to my daughter's place all I had to do was drop it off at the closest rental store and leave the keys in it. He said he filled it up with gas so that I wouldn't have to worry about replacing the gas I used. He shut the truck door. Slapped it twice, and then walked away. I sat there for a few minutes not knowing what to do. Then I started crying and put the truck in drive and drove away. I pulled over at a gas station and cried for about fifteen minutes. Afterwards, I went inside and washed my face and drove three hours to go stay with my daughter. I remember thinking that I should have seen it coming when he suggested the week before that my sixteen-year-old son should go stay with my sister or my eldest daughter who had moved to the same town my mother lived in. I didn't want to be away from him, but I knew that with my not being able to drive after the surgery that it would be safer for him to stay with my sister or daughter.

He had already been robbed by gun point and had his K-Swiss tennis shoes stolen from him inside of the school and in front of the school office. After finding out about what happened I called in work late and went to the school the next day to ask why I had not been notified, and why the police were not called. They told me they had police on site and that they had it under control. They told me that the student who robbed him had been expelled. I didn't think that was good enough. I wanted to press charges against the boy, and they told me that by doing so I would put my son in even more danger, and that there was no reason to cause a panic with bad publicity. I was furious. I wanted them to call the police so that I could press charges against them for not protecting my child. They refused to call the police, and they assured me that my son was safe. Well, I filed complaints, and had him transferred to a better school.

However, after what had happened, I didn't want him to be at the mercy of missing the school bus for functions at school or anything else and have to walk home.   So, I had to put his safety first and allow him to go stay with my sister. I missed him terribly and felt like I had failed him. We were always close, and I felt like I should have found a different way to handle the situation. I tried to think positive about the situation that had just unfolded by thinking that at least I would be closer to my children. However, that did not keep me from feeling like I had been blindsided. I had just given my boyfriend over twenty-seven-hundred-dollars to help cover expenses for my son and I while I recovered from the surgery just a few days before he felt like my son needed to go stay with family because I wouldn't be able to drive him to or from school if he needed me to. It was like having someone spit in my face. It was three times the amount that I normally paid for my share of expenses, but if I had to have chemotherapy, I wanted to make sure that my children and I were not a burden on him.

That was how I got repaid. Cold. Real cold. I was glad I found out how cold he was before I married him instead of finding out afterwards. It hurt so bad that it completely changed how I felt about him. I called my surgeon's assistant and told her what happened and asked if she could have the surgery postponed because I wasn't going to have a place to stay near the hospital after being released, and no one in my family was able to drive me there and go back to get me. She told me that after my having the biopsy I needed to have my surgery as soon as possible. Then she told me not to worry about not having a place to stay after I got out of the hospital, and for me to have my surgery and the social worker at the hospital would help me find a place to go to if no one was there to pick me up when it was time for me to be released. I knew she was right, so I agreed to be there for my surgery as scheduled.

The night before my surgery I drove back to Little Rock and sat in my car in the parking lot holding a cigarette in my hand. I was looking at it in the light of the security lights above me. I knew that one way or another that was going to be the last cigarette I was ever going to smoke. So, at 11:50 pm I lit that cigarette, and I sat there in my car and smoked my last cigarette right up until midnight. Then I put it out and removed the ashtray. I poured water in the ashtray to make sure all the fire was out and wiped it clean with some paper towels so that I would not have to smell it when I got back into the car. I threw the paper towels away and went in to wash my hands. I spent the rest of the night in a recliner chair in a family waiting room filled with people that I didn't know. Before I fell asleep I remember wondering why I smoked that nasty cigarette, and thinking to myself that was probably why I had cancer.

THE MASTECTOMY

The next morning, I was awakened by the rustling noises of the people around me and hearing the names of people being called out to either go back for surgery, or to talk to them about a family member. I must have been exhausted the night before when I went to sleep, because I had slept right up until the time I was supposed to check in for my surgery. I was grateful that I did not oversleep and miss my name being called. I finished my registration and sat quietly by the windows looking out at the parking lot. As I sat there, I felt a little bit lonely. I guess I had hoped that my coldhearted ex would have showed up for support, but he didn't. So, I done what big girls do. I waited patiently for my turn to have my life changed forever. When I got in the back to be prepped for surgery everything at the hospital was the same as it was when I had the biopsy. Only this time it was different for me emotionally.

I remembered my family members who had died from cancer after they had surgery. The air hitting the cancer made it grow fast, and then suddenly they were gone. My mother-in-law told me that if I ever got cancer not to let them operate on me. For the first time the thought crossed my mind that I may not want to have the surgery. My ex-mother-in-law, whom I totally loved and adored, died like the others did after air hit the cancer she had. I was with my daughter in Memphis with her having a heart bypass when my ex-mother-in-law died. I couldn't leave my daughter to go back to Florida to my mother-in-law's funeral. I felt sad that I couldn't be there for the family who had always accepted me with open arms even after I divorced her son. She visited with me often after I remarried, and brought me a lot of baby clothes when I was pregnant. She was a good woman that everyone loved. She had a good heart, and I still miss her.

As I laid on the bed waiting for my turn to have surgery I could hear someone crying in one of the other units. I did not know if it was because of bad news or if they were afraid of what they may have to face. I also remembered what my uncle had taught me about God's love and power. I got on the floor next to the hospital bed and prayed to God thanking him for allowing me to find good doctors, and for guiding them and using them to remove the cancer from me. I thanked him for protecting the other patients, and for protecting and healing me, and for allowing me to live so that I could be there for my children and to help others find him. I asked God to tell my son and grandchild in Heaven that I loved them, and to tell my granddaughter that her momma missed her every day. I praised him for being the great and mighty God that he is because there is no other above him, and asked that if it were my time to die to please take care of my children and have mercy on me for my sins and weaknesses and allow me to serve him in Heaven. The nurse entered the room when I was praying, and when I said Amen, so did she. I felt peace.

They done the same thing they had done the last time and gave me a sedative to help me relax right before they took me to the surgery room, however, I don't believe I remember hearing any music playing. I do not remember much of anything about that surgery except being waken straight up in the most severe pain I had ever felt in my life! When I was taken to my hospital room from recovery a nurse started a medication drip on me that was routine for most people, but she had not paid attention to my allergy bracelet or the signs above my bed. The medicine she gave me works the opposite on me from what it is designed to do and causes me to have severe pain. So, when she put that medicine in my IV it woke me up from a deep sleep and I sat straight up screaming my lungs out! I was yelling at them to get it out, it was burning me, and I was trying to pull the IV line and the tissue expanders out of my chest by trying to claw my chest open to get them out. At first, I didn't know what was causing the pain, but I was trying to get it out.

Nurses came running in all directions and was asking the nurse with a needle still in her hand what she gave me. She told them what she gave me, and one of them yelled at her that I was allergic to it, and then she asked her why she didn't read the poster over my bed. They were literally holding me down trying to keep me from hitting them and from clawing at myself. Some man said to give me something that I didn't recognize and whatever it was it knocked me out cold within just a few seconds. When I woke up the next time, I was sore, but I did not have that fire burning pain shooting through my chest. The head nurse checked in on me to make sure I was doing okay while an Aid took my vital signs. She asked me if I remembered my surgery, and I told her no, but I remembered waking up to that nurse putting the wrong medicine in me, and that it burned so bad it felt like I had been set on fire. She told me that the nurse had been dismissed from not reading the warning posters, and for not looking at my allergies. She didn't say if dismissed meant the lady had been fired, or sent home for the day, and I didn't ask.

She apologized for my having to go through that and told me that I was going through enough without having to deal with someone not paying attention to what they were doing. She assured me that it would never happen again. They treated me like a queen my entire stay there. I don't know if it was because of the nurse messing up, or if it was just the normal thing they done there. Either way, I was safe, but still alone. My family called the nurses desk several times to check in on me, and my son insisted on talking to me. So, they had a nurse to go to my room to hand me the phone when it rang. I couldn't raise my arms up very much at all. So, I couldn't reach the phone on the nightstand. I was glad to hear my son's voice. I wanted to cry, but I didn't because I didn't want to scare him. I had to be brave. I don't know who all tried to call me, but by all the ringing going on I knew someone other than God, the doctors, and nurses cared about me.

My cancer care coordinator cared too. She visited me in the hospital, and when I told her the situation with my ex, she immediately went to work trying to find someplace for me to go when they got ready to release me. The next day she told me that she had called my ex and asked if I could stay there just for a few weeks until they could remove my drain tubes out of my chest, and he told her no. So, she planned for me to go to a nursing home. I didn't want to be in a nursing home, but I couldn't very well stay in my car out in the parking lot. Not only was it too cold, I would starve to death. I agreed to go wherever she found a place for me to go, and I thanked her for going out of her way to help me. Other than her I had an entire team of people helping me to get ready to go home.

The Physical Therapist visited with me to make sure I was able to walk, and she showed me how to exercise my arms so that my shoulders didn't lock up from holding them still too long. A counselor visited with me about grieving over the loss of my breast and told me about a support group for cancer survivors that I was welcome to attend. The Anesthesiologist checked in on me to make sure I was alert and didn't have any long-term side effects from any medication I had been given. A Preacher came to pray with me several times, and he helped me fill out my meal request card for the next day. A couple of Volunteer workers came to visit with me while I was there. They both asked if I needed them to help me with anything, and one of them asked me if I would like for her to read to me. I agreed. And as she did I fell asleep while she was reading.

I don't remember what it was she was reading. I just remember the soft sound of her voice reading the words with emotion just like it was a real conversation taking place. It came at a good time too, because I was feeling a little bit lonely and unwanted. I guess I was having a pity party. Something I never allowed myself to do, and something I still do not allow myself to do. The hospital floor doctor checked on me every day, and of course there were Student Doctors and Resident Doctors who needed to look me over and ask the same questions every day. I didn't mind though. I knew that they needed the practice so that they could finish school and help someone like me. Maybe even be able to help me one day, and if they were going to help me, I wanted them to be the best they could be. So, I didn't mind them poking and squeezing and asking a hundred questions. They were all nice, and none of them made me feel like a guinea pig or like a pin cushion.

My Plastic Surgeon visited with me every day to check my tissue expanders. He explained to me that it would not be possible to get the size implants we had discussed about in his office. He told me there was not enough of my chest wall left to stretch far enough to get implants for a size "D". He was certain though that he could stretched me out enough to get a size "C" for me. He told me that I would have to see him every week and that he would start the stretching procedure as soon as my chest wall healed enough for him to do it. Normally it would only take a couple of weeks or a month, but in my case it could be longer. And of course, the star doctor made his appearance several times. My Breast Oncologist Surgeon. I felt like I had won the lottery when I found that doctor. He never once gave me the feeling that he was in it for the money. He never made any inappropriate remarks or uncaring body language movements that said I was annoying him. He always took time to listen to me. Not to mention the bonus hug I got every time I seen him that made me feel like he seen me as a human worth saving. After what I had been through that alone meant a lot to me, and it helped to keep my spirits up. Especially when he told me the bad news.

Before my surgeon broke the bad news to me about how bad the cancer was, I had already received a tip from my plastic surgeon when he told me about how I didn't have enough chest wall left to stretch out for size "D" implants. I wondered why, but I didn't ask. I was still a little weak, and not clear headed enough from the medicine they were giving me for the pain for me to focus on what he meant by that. Later that day I found out what he meant by "not enough chest wall left." My breast surgeon told me that even though the cancer was slow growing, because of my having it for so long it had spread into my chest wall. He told me that he had to remove part of my chest wall to get it all. He also told me that he had to take out the surrounding lymph nodes to make sure the cancer had not spread to them, and that my immune system would be weak from not having as many lymph nodes as before the surgery.

There was some good news though. The good news was that even though there was no guarantee that he got all the cancer, because sometimes it could be so microscopic small that it can't be seen with the eye, he was almost certain that by taking part of my chest wall and some of my lymph nodes that he was able to get it all. He told me that he felt confident enough to say that I was cancer free. I felt a wave of relief go over my body, and I felt blessed to finally have a doctor that cared enough to make sure that I was cancer free. I'm not saying that the other doctors didn't care, what I am saying is that he was one of those exceptional few that take the extra steps in their job to get to the root of the problem. Just like the doctor who laid out all of those books for me to study so that I would have a fighting chance so live.

The day came for me to leave the hospital. I felt a little weak and drowsy from the pain medicine they gave me to help with my traveling from the hospital. My Cancer Care Coordinator was there to pick me up and take me to the nursing home she had planned for me to go to. It was supposed to last for a few weeks until I was able to get the drain tubes removed, and then return to my daughter's place in northeast Arkansas. But that didn't happen.

When we arrived, I recognized the place from seeing it while driving and while riding on the city bus. It had been a cheap motel in the past that had two stories and two buildings facing each other. It had a bad reputation for being a flop house for prostitutes and drug dealers. It was right down the road from the jail house, but there was always extra street activity going on in front of it.

My ex told me one day when we were going down the road and seen people outside of it that it had been closed down by the city and had been reopened as a facility for disable people to live who could not take care of themselves. He said that it was just a cover for drug dealers. I don't know how true that is, but after what I went through it made me wonder if he was right. There was supposed to be a nurse on site in case there was an emergency, but the nurse had quit, and had not been replaced. I sat in the car while my caseworker checked me in at the office, and she then helped me to the room. She told me that she didn't like what she saw, and that she was going to try to find me somewhere else to go. When we reached my downstairs room there was a puddle of what looked and smelled like fresh vomit right in front of my doorway. My caseworker had to help me over it, and when we entered the room I tried to turn around and walk out.

There was a woman in the room sitting on a bed on the opposite side of the room who obviously was severely mentally disabled, and who was agitated over us being in her room telling us that we needed to leave. My caseworker told her that she had a new roommate, and that I was a nice lady she would like. The lady had been setting on the bed I was supposed to use, and my caseworker told her I didn't feel well and needed to lay down on my bed. The lady stopped yelling at us and went to her own side of the room. My caseworker helped me over to my bed and sat down my belongings. She checked the bathroom to make sure there was running water and said that she would have the office send someone to clean it for me. There was a metal shelf for a closet, and a small dirty ugly brown nightstand with peeling paint next to my twin size bed with no telephone.

There was only one light, and it was the ceiling light with the switch being next to the door on the opposite side of the room. There were no locks on the door, and no chain on the inside. Anyone could walk in from outside at any time. My caseworker helped me get in bed and told me that she would be right back. The bed was hard, and I could feel the bed springs through the mattress. It smelled like musty dirty clothes. There was only one hard flat pillow that stunk so bad I had to put my sweater over it to block the smell in order to lay my head on it. I didn't want to lay my head on it at all, but the pain medicine had me sleepy, and I nodded out while trying not to breath in deep so I wouldn't get sick from the smell. I could still smell the bed clothes, but I fell asleep anyway. A few minutes later she returned and seemed upset about something.

She told me that there was no nurse there to control medication, and that she did not want to leave it on my bed side table like the lady in the office told her to do. She said the place needed to be condemned and that she was going to report the place to have it closed. She told me to rest and she would be back to check on me, and she promised me that she was going to get me out of there even if she had to take me home with her when she got off work. She left and went back to work. The room was dark, and I could hear the sounds of people talking outside in the courtyard, but I was too sleepy to stay awake and wait for her to return. When she checked on me during her lunch break the vomit was still in front of my door, and when she entered my room, to my understanding she caught the other lady who I shared the room with next to my bed with me still sleeping, with my medicine bottles in her hands.

I woke up to my caseworker telling the lady to give her the bottles. She told me to stay awake and she would be right back. She went to the front office to complain, but there was no one there to complain to. The office was closed for lunch. When she returned to my room, she found that I had fell back asleep and my roommate was going through my suitcase. My caseworker made her leave my stuff alone. She woke me up telling me what had happened and asked me for my cell phone. She looked up my ex-boyfriend's phone number on my phone and called him from her cell phone. She told him that she was the lady who had spoken to him a few days earlier, and told him how she had to take me to a fraudulent nursing home, and that people were stealing my medication and going through my belongs. Then she told him she felt like it was not safe for me to be there. He told her to call my daughter.

She told him, "No." And told him that my daughter lived too far away from the hospital, and that I needed to be close to the doctor for a few weeks. My caseworker was a strong woman that refused to let me be mistreated. She told him that she did not care rather or not he wanted to be with me; she just wanted to inform him that after the stunt he pulled kicking me out just days before my having a lifesaving surgery that if he did not get over there and pick me up and take me home she was going to file a report for his arrest for medical neglect. She reminded him that he had made the mistake of giving me a receipt for the money I had given him for mine and my son's expenses, and that counted as a rent receipt and he had until five pm to pick me up and take me home with him and care for me or the police would be knocking at his door. She told him that she was sending home health care nurses to check on me every day, and that he had better make sure that I had what I needed.

Then she told him where I was located at and ended the call. I told her that she probably just made him mad, and that I doubt he would show up. She told me not to worry. She would be there to make sure he did, or she was going to call the police just like she told him she would. She sat with me in the room for over an hour until the lady in the front office returned from her lunch break. She helped me walk to the office with my belongings and told the lady what she found. She also told her that she wanted me to set in the office until my ride picked me up early that evening, and that she would be back to check on me. The lady protested, and my caseworker told her real quick that it would only take her about fifteen minutes to have that place closed down and her arrested. The lady said she just worked there, she didn't own the place, but she would let me set there until the office closed at five. If my ride wasn't there by then I would have to wait outside.

He showed up about four-thirty that afternoon and helped me get in his truck. He never said one word to me until after we got inside of his place. He told me that he had a new roommate, so I couldn't stay in the spare bedroom. He told me that I would have to sleep in the same room with him, but it would be okay. He took my suitcase to the back bedroom, and then left. He was gone all night, and I never seen or heard his roommate that night either. Later that night I was hungry and tried to walk to the kitchen to find something to eat. I had to hang on to the walls to keep my balance. No one told me that losing my breast would cause me to have balance issues. I couldn't find anything simple to eat, so I helped myself to making a small hamburger patty without bread. I cleaned my mess and went back to bed. The next morning my arms, chest, and between my shoulder blades was throbbing.

I could not take the pain medicine they had given me because the bottle was empty. I assumed that the lady who I shared a room with within that so-called nursing home took my medicine. So, I took some generic acetaminophen and fixed myself some breakfast. About an hour later my home health nurse showed up. She took my vital signs, extracted the fluid out of my drain bulbs and replaced my bandages. She watched me do my arm exercises to make sure my arms were not locking up. I needed help doing the exercises because my arms were already trying to lock up from not being able to move them very much. Afterwards, she helped me to the bathroom to clean up. Because I still could not use my arms very well I had not taken a shower yet because there was no one there to help me. I could not reach my backside to clean myself very good, and even though I felt embarrassed, I knew it needed to be done, so I allowed her to help me. I was so embarrassed that I wanted to cry. I never thought about needing help like that when I was asking for that mammogram. I had not been prepared for it.

That evening my ex showed up after he got off work. He seen that I was trying to make supper and helped me finish cooking. I met his roommate just about the time supper was done. It was a man that he worked with who I always thought did not like my ex because of the way he popped out hateful remarks when I was around him. As it turned out, that was just his attitude toward everything. We all ate supper and watched television together, and then my ex cleaned the kitchen for me. That night my ex told me that he didn't want to bump my chest, and that he was going to sleep on the sofa in the living room. I was grateful because I truly was sore. He let me sleep in the next morning. I never heard a peep when he got ready for work. When I did wake up, I was so sore I could barely move. The muscles in my back were tight. I knew I needed a warm shower to help them relax.

So, after I fixed myself breakfast, I cut wholes in a big black trash bag to represent a T-shirt to put my head and arms through so I could take a shower. I got the small plastic stool out of the kitchen closet that I normally used as a step stool to reach things in the top cabinets, and I put it in the bathtub so that I could set on it and let the water run on my back. A few at a time I gathered face towels, hand towels, and bath towels to make sure I had everything I needed. The plan was to wrap a hand towel around my neck so that water would not run down my neck inside the trash bag and onto my bandages. I got the roll of paper medical tape, sandwich bags to put over the drain tube holes going into my body, the hand towel to put around my neck, and laid the bath towels close to the bathtub so that I could reach them easily. Then came the moment of truth.

As I slowly undressed in the bathroom, I wasn't paying attention to the mirrors over the sink counter or on the door. After I got undressed, I reached for the tape and sandwich bags to put over the drain tube holes and got a glimpse of my body in the mirror. I looked frail and pale. I stood there looking at myself in the mirror over the sink and realized that my chest was shaped different. I had been wearing a surgical bra that clearly had been too tight on me, but I couldn't feel a thing. My chest looked flat under it, and the bandages sticking out from under it in all directions looked damp. I thought to myself that I must have done some sweating in my sleep, and that I couldn't leave them on wet like that. So, after I took the bra off, I slowly removed the bandages. What I saw broke my heart, and nearly made me pass out. Literally. I got lightheaded and dizzy and had to grabbed and hang on to the countertop to keep from falling. I sat down on the toilet seat and almost went into a full-blown hyperventilating panic attack.

I cupped my hands over my mouth and breathed into them like you would a small paper bag. Then I remembered my grandmother telling people to put their head between their knees to help with dizziness, so I sat down in the bathroom floor with my knees up and I laid my head between my knees. Within a couple of minutes, I felt better, but I just sat there. I did not want to look behind me at the mirror on the door, and I did not want to stand up and see myself in the mirror over the sink. I sat there thinking, "I'm alive. Whatever it is I see it is me, and I'm okay. I'm still alive." I slowly stood up while looking at the floor. I held onto the sink counter, and with a deep breath I looked up at myself in the mirror. What I saw looked like something in the movies. Like a dead person's body in a morgue that had been cut up and stitched back together in different directions with stitches making smiling faces at me on both sides of my chest. I didn't have nipples anymore.

There were only stitches and the drain tubes half full of blood sewn into my skin to keep them from sliding out of my body. There were two soft plastic bulbs holding blood dangling at the end those tubes. One hanging from under my arm on one side and one hanging under my chest on the other side. I stood there staring at myself. My chest was raised up just a little on each side. Like dirt that had been swept under a rug. When I touched my skin where my pretty little breast use to be it felt like rubber to my fingers, but I could not feel a thing on my chest. I started crying thinking no wonder my ex didn't want me anymore. I sat back down on the toilet seat and pulled myself together. I said to myself, "This is no time to have a pity party. I have to get myself in that shower so the water can run down on my muscles and help them relax. Clearly no one is here to help me, so I have to put my imaginary big girl panties on and get it done by myself."

I went back to the counter and while avoiding looking at the mirror I cleaned around my wounds from the surgery, replaced the bandages, and gently taped the sandwich bags over the holes in my body that the drain tubes were dangling from. I realized that the towel around my neck was not going to work good enough to keep water off my chest. So I cut the trash bag up in a rectangle shape and taped it over my entire chest area. I slowly got into the bathtub and fixed the water temperature just the way I liked it. I didn't think about the cold water that was going to shoot out from the shower head before the warm water could come out of it. When I pulled that knob up for the shower to come on, I nearly jumped out of my skin! That water was so cold that it felt like I had jumped into a tub full of ice water. Instantly my chest muscles drew up tight and hurt from deep within.

That was the first time of many times that I had muscle contractions from my chest being too cold. The muscles in my chest would contract from the cold air, or water, and it would squeeze the implants in my chest, and cause pressure and pain deep inside my chest. To this day the implants act like thermos bottles that retain heat and cold for hours. I have to be careful not to expose myself to harsh weather, or inside temperatures, to keep myself from having a heat stroke or from getting hyperthermia. It's something they warn you about before getting the implants, but you cannot imagine what it is actually like until you have to go through it. The water finally warmed up, and I was able to sit there and relax with the water running down on my back. After I washed, dried, and dressed myself I decided that I wasn't going to ever let a man look at me again. I didn't like what I saw. So, how was a man going to be attracted to me with all those scars and no nipples. I tried to look at people beyond their physical appearance, but who would see me as anything but a bad investment?

The next week I went in to see both my Surgeon Oncologist and my Plastic Surgeon. My Surgeon Oncologist had the Pathology test results back. I had Invasive Ductal Carcinoma. Not only was it in my left side, there were traces of it in the right breast too. So, it was a good thing that we removed both breasts. If I had not asked him to remove both breast at the same time I would have had to go through it all over again within just a few months. He told me that the cancer was hormone related, and that since he believed he got all of the cancer he did not think I would have to have extensive Chemotherapy, but to make sure he was going to send me to a different type of Oncologist who specialized in different types of cancer treatments. His specialty was just seeing if it was cancer in the breast and removing it surgically if possible. His assistant couldn't get me in to see the other doctor right away. She was in demand so much that I had to wait for a couple of weeks to get in to see her. As for my Plastic Surgeon, he said that my chest wall wasn't stretching as well as he had hoped it would, and that I had to wait a few more weeks before starting the expansion process to give my chest longer time to heal.

RECOVERING AFTER THE MASTECTOMY

A couple of weeks went by with my staying with my ex and his roommate. They were nice to me, but he was barely at home. I suspected that he was seeing someone else, but I never asked him about it because it was no longer any of my business. Besides, I didn't want him to see me the way I was. That idea didn't work very well for very long. One day he came in from work early while I was in the shower. As I was trying to get out of the shower, I lost my balance and fell. I don't know what scared me worse. My falling or him barging into the bathroom to help me up out of the bathtub. I was scared, but I didn't see any blood. I couldn't tell if everything inside me was still in the right place or not because other than a constant pressure I couldn't feel a thing in my chest. As he helped me up, he seen the trash bag contraption on my chest. He dried me off, and then slowly started taking the tape off me.

I tried to protest, but he said, "Shush." So, I stood there and let him take the plastic off of my chest. I heard him gasp, and then he picked me up and carried me to the bedroom and put me in bed. I expected him to walk away, but instead he took his shirt off and laid in bed next to me. Just holding me close. I broke down crying in his chest, and he held me until I fell asleep. When I woke up, he had already fixed dinner for us, and was telling me that my food was ready and that our favorite show was on television. I laughed that night for the first time since my son left to go stay with my eldest daughter. After that he was more sensitive towards me and stopped staying out all night. He made sure that I had money for taxicabs to go to my doctors' appointments, took me shopping to buy me some clothes that fit better than what I had been wearing, and he and his friend went to the hospital to get my car for me.

The home health nurses still made visits to see me until my Surgical Oncologist removed the drain tubes from my chest. When he removed them, it didn't hurt like I thought it would. There was a mild pinching feeling, then I could feel the plastic tubes inside of me sliding out, and then there was a weird feeling like my insides were being pulled out as he gently pulled the tubes out one at a time. As he removed the tubes he cleaned the areas and put butterfly strips over each hole. He told me to keep it dry for about a week, and to return in about a month. It felt so good to have those tubes out of me. I didn't have that constant pinching and pulling feeling deep inside of me from my clothes rubbing agains the tubes when I moved. As much as I appreciated him I was glad to get a least a small break from seeing doctors, because not having to go back to see him in one months' time also gave me a little since of freedom and lifted my spirits from knowing that soon it would all just be a memory of the past. However, I did have to keep seeing the plastic surgeon every week. When the time came for him to be able to start the stretching process on me, I nearly ran from the room.

I had always been needle shy, and suddenly there was this huge syringe about two or three fingers in width with a long thick needle sticking out of it in his hand about a foot over me pointing straight down towards my chest! He had marked a spot on my chest to inject the needle, but he didn't tell me that he was going to have to stab me with it. He told me not to move, and then with one fast and hard stabbing motion he shoved the needle in the marked area on my chest! I could hear a pop, and the pressure inside was so strong that it felt like he had hit me with his fist. One at a time he slowly injected the fluid from the syringe into the tissue expanders inside my chest wall until they couldn't hold any more fluid. My chest felt tight, and it was hard to breath in deep. I told him how it felt, and he told me that it would relax in a few days and then it would be easier on me. He wanted to see me the next week to do it again. Let me tell you something. I almost did not go back to see him. I wanted to go to someone else and ask them to take those things out of me.

Then I remembered his telling me in the beginning that the process was painful, but it got easier with time, and I remembered my promising him that I would stick with it. So, I stuck with it. The next week when I returned to see him, he told me that my chest wall was not expanding like it should, and that he suspected it was because part of it had been removed in the surgery. He told me that it would be okay and that it was just going to take longer than he had anticipated. At that point he told me to return in two weeks to give it time to relax more. When I went back it was easier to breath, but it still had not relaxed enough for him to add more to them. So, I had to wait an extra two weeks to be punched in the chest again. I was in no hurry to go through that again, but the sooner he got my chest wall expanded for implants the sooner it would be over and I would be able to get back to my children.

In the meantime, I took the advice of a couple of doctors and nurses and my ex-boyfriend; I sought out help to file a complaint against the doctor who refused to have a mammogram done on me, and to file suit against him. He would not even look at my breast, the symptoms were very visual, yet he refused to exam my breast or to have test done on me. He even noted so in my medical records. If that wasn't bad enough, he insulted me for wanting the test done by calling me a hypochondriac and telling me that I was just being paranoid. Well, I made a mistake and hired an ex-nurse who said she used to work for cancer doctors, and that she went to law school to help protect patients from doctors like that. She agreed to take my case and had me to sign paperwork agreeing not to hire anyone else to represent me on the case.

Well, almost two years went by, and I had made repeated not returned phone calls trying to find out why she had not filed a claim for me with the state, and then went back to her office because I could not reach her on the phone. She was gone. I turned to the Bar Association to report her, and they told me that there were several other people who had the same complaint. She was under investigation for ethical reasons. As it turns out this lady had learned that one simple little word would give her power to completely control your case and to be able to accept payment for you from the person you filed a complaint about and be able to keep all of it for "investigating" the case for you. I found out that she was supposed to have been paid three-hundred-thousand-dollars by the doctor she was supposed to be representing me to file a claim against. She held the case up so that it would not be filed within the two-year time limit it had to be filed.

She also kept all of the money he settled out of court with without as much as a note or phone call to me. I found out about the money when his secretary refused to let me have medical records for one of my doctors by telling me to get my attorney to give me a copy of them because they paid her three-hundred-thousand-dollars for me so she should be able to give them to me and then hung up on me. That's when I went to her closed up office location. I don't know if the doctor paid her off to keep her from filing the case against him, or if he thought I got the money they gave her to give me. Either way, that lady was gone. Gone to con someone else down the road. The Legal Bar Association did nothing to help me. Instead I was told that I had two choices. I could file an application to have them "investigate" her activity with my case and report their findings to the Board of Ethics, or I could hire an attorney and file a complaint against her without their report. I could not do both. It had to be one or the other. It seemed like another scam for deep pockets. Makes you wonder if they too got paid not to file a complaint against someone. Anyway, I wish I had listened to my instinct and not hired anyone to do anything about it. It's bad business to sue a doctor. They all know about it, and some would be upset over it or may avoid caring for you for fear of you filing a complaint against them.

I know accidents happen, and I do not believe in filling against someone just because of an accident. In my opinion someone has to be obviously negligent who refuses to do what needs to be done that would cause harm to someone before they should be sued. I do not believe it is right to hold someone accountable for what someone else does unless that someone knew of the danger that could cause harm to someone. For example, in the past when I was in my twenties, I ate a piece of candy that had wood pieces in it. Of course, I did not know that the wood was in it, so when I swallowed it the candy got stuck in my throat. I was lucky that it was only a small bite, and did not choak me to death, but I was coughing and wheezing. I did not have a telephone and I had to go to the gas station that was a couple of blocks away to get help. I was taken by ambulance to the nearest hospital, and they had to do surgery on me to remove splinters in my throat. The lab report showed that the wood in the candy had been something that happened in the factory.

So, at the advice of others I took it to an attorney to file a claim for my hospital bill to be paid by the company. He told me that he couldn't take my case until after he seen if his law firm represented the candy company. They had a large list of clients, and if they had represented the candy company in the past, he could not represent me. He told me to return the next week and he would let me know what steps I needed to take. I returned the next week like I was told to and found out that the law firm he worked for could not take the case.

However, he told me that he was authorized to offer me ten thousand dollars for my inconvenience. I told him that I just wanted the hospital bill paid, and he could keep the rest. He looked like he had won a jackpot, and my ex-husband looked like he had lost one. I loved that candy. It was not the candy companies' fault that something went wrong. It wasn't like they neglected or abused me on purpose. So, I felt like it would have been wrong to take the money, and signed paperwork for the attorney to keep the money. It wasn't like the man done what this so-called attorney done to me to purposely prevent my case from being filed. He was honest. He got ten thousand dollars for his honesty. Some may think that was crazy of me to do that. Well to them it may seem crazy, but to me I was more worried about my eternal soul from taking money from someone who did not purposely neglect or hurt me.

Another example was when my first-born son died because he was too premature and I had fallen down a steep set of stairs that broke my water two weeks before my labor started. I was young, and did not know that when your water breaks you go to the hospital rather you have started having contractions or not. A family member said they called the doctor and the doctor said for me to go to the hospital when my contractions were five minutes apart. The contractions did not start for two weeks. When they did start the pain was so sharp it sent me to my knees. During a long painful labor and dry birth my baby died while I was having him. Later the report I got stated that the kidney medication I had taken when I was pregnant with him deteriorated his kidneys. The doctor told me my son would not have lived to be six months old if he had lived. He told me he was sorry. I knew that he was a great doctor, and that he would never purposely do anything to hurt me or my baby because he had taken good care of me. It was not his fault I kept kidney infections during my pregnancy, or that the medicine he gave me had side effects that the company did not give warnings for. I never thought of even trying to bring a lawsuit against him.

But this doctor refused repeatedly not to do a test I needed and insulted me for my asking him to have the mammogram done on me without even looking at my breast. The test was a free test for high risk patients. So it wasn't like I was asking for something unreasonable. So, I agreed that he needed a wakeup call so he would not be so quick to neglect, ignore, and mistreat people for asking for help. Do you want to know what the kicker to the story is? I told the lady I only wanted him to pay for the price of my mastectomy and her fee. It wasn't his fault that I had gotten cancer, but it was his fault that he refused to examine me and test me for it and insulted me for asking him to do what he went to college for years to do. By doing so it allowed the cancer to spread as bad as it had. Maybe if he had the test done on me the cancer would not have been invasive when I had the lumpectomy and the surgeon may have been able to save my breast. I lived in a small town at the time, and because of insurance and transportation I could not go just anyplace to ask a different doctor to do it, so the burden of eliminating possible cancer was on him. He paid her three-hundred-thousand-dollars to make it go away! I think if I was him, I would have rather paid for my patients' mastectomy instead of paying some greedy ex-nurse all that money to con the person that had already been physically and emotionally hurt by him. Go figure.

During that time, I met the other Breast Oncologist. She was very nice, and she didn't think I needed regular chemotherapy, but she did want me to take a hormonal replacement type of chemotherapy to keep the cancer from coming back. All I had to do was take one pill a day for five years. The catch was that it caused Uterine Cancer. I asked why I should trade one cancer for another, and she told me that breast cancer spreads, but Uterine Cancer did not spread. She told me that all I had to do was get a hysterectomy and it would solve the problem. I thought to myself, "Oh, that's all?" I'm sure she could tell what I was thinking because she explained to me that I needed the hormone replacement medicine because the cancer I had was spread into my chest wall. She told me that without the medicine I had a high chance of it reoccurring. She told me that with the medicine I had less than a five percent chance of it reoccurring. Then she told me that I would most likely be able to keep my ovaries so I wouldn't go into full menopause. But that would be up to my Gynecologist. She gave me a prescription, and some pamphlets to read about the medicine, and told me to return to see her in one months' time so she could check my blood to make sure my liver was handling the medicine without any complications.

When I left her office I looked at the pamphlets that she gave me. For some reason I did not feel well about taking that medicine. I didn't think it was possible, but as I got the medicine filled I started missing my children even worse than I missed them before I had seen her. My getting back to my children seemed like it was getting further and further away. I had to add another doctor and surgery on my list of things to do, and I had not seen my children since the day before my surgery. I missed them all and felt like I had abandoned them. By this time all three of my children were living together in my eldest daughter's apartment not far from where my mother and sisters lived. I talked to them almost every day, but it wasn't the same as being with them. My son had above average grades, but he started missing school, and I was notified by the school that they reported him to the state and that I would have to go to court to prove that I was having medical procedures done because it had been reported to them that I had abandoned him.

Well, that did not set well with me at all. I got statements from neighbors, school teachers, doctors, friends, and family stating that my son lived with me right up until the week before I could not work due to having surgery. I had money order receipts proving that I was sending money to care for him and his needs, and payroll and insurance records showing that I had insurance on him all his life. I got copies of my medical reports, and doctor visit summaries, and took them to court with me on the day my son had to be there. The accusations against me were dropped, and my son was given another chance to get his school attendance in line. I was warned that even though it was not my fault that I could not be there to care for him, if he had any more unexcused absences I would have to pay a five hundred dollar fine, and he would be put on probation until he finished high school or turned eighteen, whichever one came first. We were all relieved that was over. It was good to be able to see my children for a few days, but it was time to get back to getting my health taken care of so that I could be back with my family permanently. Besides, my ex was beginning to act like he didn't want to be an ex anymore. I wanted to get my medical stuff taken care of before he decided to kick me out again because of my not being emotionally the same towards him as I was before the surgery. I didn't have transportation to go back and forth so far to see the doctors, so I had to make my situation work until I was able to go home and get a job so I could take care of myself and my son.

I just couldn't allow myself to feel the same way about him after he kicked me out like he did before the surgery. Even though he had been sending money to my sister and daughter for me to help support my son, helped me with transportation to my medical appointments, and made sure I had what I needed it was not the same as it was before that day he loaded my stuff in that rental truck. He was no longer my hero. Instead, in the back of my head I told myself he was probably covering his butt over my giving him all that money to cover our expenses. I found out that he had a lawsuit going on over a legal issue he had in the past, and I assumed that he was just trying to make himself look good. I still loved him. I couldn't help it. But it was a sad sort of love because it felt like I could no longer trust him to stand by my side. He had a lot of good qualities, but I knew that I had no future with him because I did not fit in his plans, and I did not have that submissive type of love for him anymore. He stole it from me. Just like my ex before him had.

I finally saw the Gynecologist I was referred to. She too was friendly, and she had CT Scans done on me that showed I had fibroid tumors in my uterus. Not just one, but several of them, and a couple of them were very large. That explained why my stomach felt sore all the time. Fibroid tumors seldom turn cancerous, but with my needing to take the hormone replacement therapy and the large fibroid tumors that most likely would get larger, it was clear that a hysterectomy was needed. But, while the billing company for the doctor was waiting for approval from the insurance company my doctor had an accident, and it put my surgery on hold. I was glad that it didn't kill her and felt bad for her going through such pain. I liked her, and trusted her, so I decided to wait for her to go back to work to have the surgery done. After six months my stomach was looking like I was pregnant, and my monthly cycles were extremely heavy, so I decided that maybe I needed to have someone else do the surgery if she couldn't do it in the near future.

I called her office to see if she was back at work yet, and that's when I found out that she had broken her back in the accident, and that she was still off work for rehabilitation. Her receptionist told me that it wasn't a complete break, and that she planned on returning to work within the year. I asked her how she would be abe to do surgery on me if her back was broken. She told me that the doctor was able to stand, but she would have to have supports to hold her in place, and told me not to worry, it would be fine. I told her to pass along my get well wishes and told her I would call her in a few months. My condition got worse, and even though I liked her, she couldn't help me. I needed help before she could get back to work. So, I tried to switch doctors. What I found out was that my insurance had already approved her to do my surgery and had already paid her for it. The check they sent to her was not returned. So, it could not be done by anyone other than her unless she closed down her business, that was being ran by her Nurse Practitioner, or she had not done my surgery within a years' time. At that point the doctor would have to refund them the money for them to pay someone else to do it. They told me that I could always take her to court and force her to pay for another doctor to do my surgery since she had already been paid for it, but I felt like that was unnecessary. I was sure that she had enough to deal with without dealing with something like that on top of it. I was sure that it was a billing error on her billing company's part. So, it did not get done.

GRANDMA DIED

I talked to my grandmother at least several times a week. As far as food was concerned, she would guide me about what to do or not to do. She gave me the impression that she felt useful and needed by going out of her way to make sure I was fallowing my diet. She wanted to know about all of my doctor visits, and any test results I had. She herself was having Chemotherapy treatments every week. It helped her by feeling needed by me. In return I felt needed by her. I remember waking up one morning feeling like something was wrong with her. I tried for two days to call her, but no one was answering the phone. I could not get hold of anyone. So, I called the hospital. She was in the hospital. I was able to talk to her the night before she died. She told me that God told her it was time to go and for me not to be mad. I started crying and reminded her that she needed to be positive like she told me to do.

She told me cancer wasn't the problem. The problem was that her and my step-grandfather both had gotten a bad staph infection in their groan area from a home health care aid who had treated someone with staph before she went to their house. Her immune system was weak from the cancer treatments, and the infection was so bad that she had to have surgery that next day, and she was afraid that with all the problems she had been having that she wouldn't make it out of surgery. The only thing she was worried about was my eldest uncle. He had severe speech problems and was mildly mentally delayed from an accident when he was younger. Grandma was concerned that my uncle would not be able to take care of himself if she died. Then she changed the subject, and asked me about my day. We talked, laughed about a few memories, and cried about a few more memories, and then we prayed. She told me that sooner or later she was going to have to go be with the Lord, and that when that time came for me not to be mad at God because he had been good to her. I promised I wouldn't.

She died that next day from a blood clot that had set up from the surgery she had. At the exact time she was supposed to have died I could feel something was wrong. I felt a rush go through me and a since of urgency. Someone needed help, but who? I didn't know where to turn to help whoever it was that needed help.When I found out from my sister-in-law what happened I almost died. I felt like someone ripped my heart right out of my chest. I hurt for her, and prayed that she did not suffer. She was a great lady, and I felt guilty for not being there to help her. I felt like she was the only person on earth who understood how I was feeling, and the only one who cared. I lost my best friend that day. I started to get mad, then I remembered the promise I made to her, and realized that she knew God was telling her it was time to go home to be with him. I still miss her, and every time I attend a cancer event I walk or demonstrate a flag in her honor.

I STARTED A CANCER TREATMENT

During all this time I still had not started the hormone replacement therapy. I read the information that came with the medicine, and it just felt wrong to me. For some reason my instinct told me not to take it. As far as I could tell I wasn't allergic to the ingredients, but it seemed too much like birth control pills, and I had problems every time I had tried them. Birth control medicines made my chest hurt within days, and my legs would hurt like someone had broken them. The doctor told me I could not take them because I was at high risk of setting up blood clots. In the past I had to be put on blood thinners for a couple of weeks to stop the pain. I did not want to go through that again. But after having another visit with my Breast Oncologist, who was clearly upset with me for not trying it, I decided to try it like she asked me too. I was supposed to take one tablet in the morning. But when I did, I felt weird all day afterwards. I called the Pharmacist, and he told me to skip the next morning dose, and to take it at bedtime instead.

That way I would sleep through the side effects while my body was adjusting to the medicine. I done like he told me to, and I felt better the next day. I did not have that foggy brain feeling. Within a few days I was full of energy, and I felt like a spring chicken. I had not felt that good in years. I felt that way for a couple of weeks. Then without realizing it my energy got less and less over the next week. One day I woke up and my ex told me I needed more sun because I looked a little pale. He was right. I was so white I almost looked see through. But who cared? Not me. My skin was clear and I looked younger. I was loving it. I couldn't understand why I hadn't tried that medicine in the beginning like I was asked to. But, a couple of days later I woke up looking greyish and I was feeling sick to my stomach. I went in the restroom to wash my face and brush my teeth. Blood started pouring out of my mouth like I had been hit in the mouth or had a tooth pulled. When I spit a tooth flew into the sink. I was horrified! It was my top front side tooth.

I had read the warning pamphlet that came with the medicine. I knew it was one of the possible side effects, but it didn't make me feel any better knowing that my beautiful smile was gone forever. I thought about calling the doctor. But it was the weekend and because of my history of having anxiety, and the one doctor thinking I was paranoid for thinking I was sick, I decided to wait until the next morning when the doctor's office would be open. I didn't want to seem anxious, and I really did not want another hospital bill on top of the ones I already had. I was depressed and embarrassed over my tooth. So, I went to bed for the rest of the day. By that night my heart was racing and seemed like it was going a hundred to nothing. Nothing I done would help. My chest hurt and I had a hard time breathing. I had no one there with me to take me to the emergency room, and I didn't know if it was anxiety causing it over my tooth falling out, or if my body was rejecting the medicine I was taking. I did not want an ambulance bill over an anxiety attack.

So, I laid propped up on my left side and waited until the doctor's office opened to call them. It was that way all night long. I had the telephone in my hand waiting for the minuet they opened to call them . They were quick to act and told me to go straight to the emergency room. I had no one there to drive me. So, I had to take an ambulance anyway. They done a CT Scan and gas test on my lungs to see if I had built up a blood clot. It was a rare but possible side effect. I did not have a blood clot, but because of the side effects I was having they told me to stop taking the medicine. I had only been on the medicine for twenty-one days, and that twenty-one days took a big toll on my body. There was another medication that I could take, but I had to be menopausal for a year before I could take it. I wasn't menopausal, and It seemed as though I had a blood clotting issue that put me at high risk for standard type treatments. So, I was left in limbo. Right then and there other than having occasional surgeries when tumors and lymph nodes got too big or painful that ended all cancer related treatments. Over the next couple of days, I lost another tooth and a toenail. I stayed locked away in my bedroom not wanting anyone to see me. It took about a week after I stopped taking the medicine to start feeling more normal. Normal for me. However, I realized after feeling good the first week of taking that medication and feeling the way I normally felt were not the same.

I did not know how much the cancer had taken out of me until I realized how I was supposed to feel. I also realized that after that my body was more sensitive to everything, and I was gaining weight like crazy. Before the cancer was removed from me, I was slim, but muscular. No matter how much I ate I did not gain any weight. I had been born premature, and I beat the odds and survived, but I was skinny my entire life except when I was pregnant. When I was pregnant, I set up gestational diabetes and toxemia and gained a lot of weight just like I was gaining then. I went from one hundred six pounds, to one-hundred seventy-eight pounds in just a matter of a few months. My body was doing the same thing with gaining weight that I had done when I was pregnant. I saw my primary care doctor every month, and at first, he thought my weight gain was due to my kidneys not working right, but the test came back almost normal.

So, it was a process of elimination to find out what the problem was. He had a series of test ran on me, and even though they were not normal, they were not off the chart and would not cause that kind of weight gain. He questioned me about my activities and what I ate every day and how much of it I ate. As soon as I said that I drank about a half-gallon of orange juice a day to keep my Vitamin C levels up he put down his clipboard, and looked at me. He asked, "How much did you say?" I told him again how much and why. He told me that there was no reason to go any further. He said that before I had the cancer removed my body had to work overtime to keep my immune system up and it caused me to be slim, but I no longer had cancer, and so I was just like everyone else and had to watch what I ate and how much of it I ate. He said my drinking that much orange juice was loading my body with unused sugar causing my body to store it for energy later. Thus, causing me to get overweight. I had not thought about that. When my ex got home that evening, I told him what the doctor said. He told me he was going to solve that problem. I was afraid that he was going to stop buying me orange juice, but instead he built me a homemade miniature step and put it on my side of the bed. He told me to step up on it twenty-five times, and then after a few days increased it to fifty times, and then one hundred times. He bought me knee pads and a helmet to ride his ten-speed bicycle and watched me while I rode it down to the corner and back. I started off making ten circles, then twenty-five, then fifty, then I increased my riding to one hundred complete circles to the corner and back to our driveway. By this time my breathing was getting better, I had more energy, I started jazzercising and kickboxing again, and I started losing weight. I got down to one-hundred-twenty-five pounds, but because of the tissue expanders my chest area was still larger than I was before. All that exercising helped my chest wall to relax enough so that my plastic surgeon was able to finish my stretching process.

It took months of painful treatments on expanding my tissue expanders in my chest wall to prepare me for breast implants. On the day I had surgery to have the tissue expanders removed, and the breast implants installed, I was excited to get the surgery behind me. No more being jabbed in the chest like I was being stabbed to death. No more tightness from having my chest wall stretched out so much that I couldn't breathe in deep, and all of it meant that I was one step closer to being able to move back home with my children. I had my ex, friend at that point, to drop me off at the hospital on his way to work. He asked if I wanted him to stay with me, but I told him I would be okay, and to go do his thing. I checked in with the receptionist as soon as she got there and sat and waited for my turn to go in the back. I sort of wish I had slept until time for my surgery like I did the last time because I was so hungry that I felt like my stomach was eating on my backbone.

My stomach was burning, and then it started growling. At first it sounded like bubbles under water in a swimming pool, but by the time they called me to the back it sounded more like an angry dog who was going to bite someone that was trying to take it's food. I was looking out the window and I saw my plastic surgeon walking up the sidewalk with a small white box in his hand that was only about the size of two of my fists overlapping each other. I assumed that was my implants. I was glad he was there, and that time was getting closer to getting it over with, but that box looked small compared to all the pain I had to go through to get what was inside of it. I wondered if it was going to be worth it. Either way, I was there, the doctor was there, it was time, and worth it or not it was going to happen. They called me to go in the back to get prepped for surgery. It was the same friendly people, and the same routine.

It seemed like once they had me on the bed, and had given me the sedative, it was over. Only this time I woke up nauseous. I didn't vomit, but I felt like I was going to. My chest felt cold, and I was shaking like an earthquake was rattling me all over the place. They had to put a heater hose blowing under my blanket to warm me up. I had no trouble waking up, and I did not have to stay in recovery long. As a matter of fact, I sat in the waiting room for several hours for my friend to get off work and pick me up to take me home. I guess someone called him because he showed up early and drove me to his place. He made sure I had everything I needed next to the bed, then he left to go back to work. I was supposed to have someone stay with me around the clock for twenty-four hours after surgery in case I had complication, but that didn't happen. I slept through the night without waking up to go to the restroom. The next morning I went in the bathroom to look at myself, and I expected to see breast. I was excited to see what I looked like, but what I found looked like a grapefruit had been cut in half and each half had been stuck inside my chest wall. Sort of like going to the beach and filling a cereal bowl with clay like sand and turning it over upside down for the small mound to sit on the flat beach.

No breast. No nipples. Just two half-moon mounds sticking out in front of my chest. Like a padded bra without the bra. Also, there was those same scares smiling at me from the first surgery just underneath them. To make it worse there were two more scars in the center of those mounds sitting on my chest that were wide and ugly like someone had ran a knife back and forth through a cake mix to get the air bubbles out. I had expected to see breast like the women I seen in magazines with implants. He had not told me what I would look like. I was so disappointed that I cried like a baby. I mean everything let loose that had been built up from the very beginning of finding out I had breast cancer. I must have cried almost an hour, or so, until I cried myself to sleep.

When I woke up I got dressed and accepted the fact that I was just going to have to accept that I looked like a freek show, and get on with my life. I was still me. My body looked different, but I was still the same person underneath those scars.

When my friend got in from work that evening, he wanted to see what they looked like. I didn't want him to see them and told him that it didn't turn out right. He wanted to see anyway. So, we went in the back, and I took off my shirt, and I could see the tears swelling up in his eyes. I told him I knew he would be disappointed and that was why I didn't want him to see what I looked like. He told me he wasn't disappointed. He was mad. He was mad that I went through all that hell just to end up looking like that. He told me that he was going to take off work and go have a talk with the doctor who done that to me. I told him to just leave it alone, and I would find someone to make me look right later down the road. Needless to say, that did not happen either. I still look the same today as I did then. I had to make a few trips back to that doctor for him to pull what looked like plastic fishing string out of my chest. He could only do one side because the other side started tearing my skin. To this day it is still in me holding that implant in tighter than the other one.

After that I decided that since I couldn't have the hysterectomy yet, I couldn't take the cancer treatment, I had my tissue expanders taken out and my two half-moon looking implants put in, I had gotten my weight under control, and I wasn't on any medications at all anymore, there was no reason for me not to go back home to be by my children. All I needed to do was find a place to stay until I could find a job and get my own place. My daughter said I could sty with her, but she had married a man who did not want me to stay with them because they could not afford to care for me. My mother had been staying with my grandmother after my father died, and then she stayed with my sister after my grandmother died. She didn't want anyone staying in her house because she felt like it was haunted after my father died at home from Leukemia. My sister said that I could stay there with them for a couple of weeks while I looked for a job to get my own place. So, I told my friend that it was time for me to go be with my children. We got into a bad argument because he told me what I wasn't going to do, and I straight up told him that he couldn't tell me what to do. I got mad and said, "Watch me!" Then I walked out of the door. I had never talked to him like that before and it shocked him. He tried to keep me from leaving as I was walking out of the door, and a push pull kind of thing happened, and that was the end of that. I called someone and asked them to buy me a bus ticket home and left the next day.

SUPER STRENGTH

I got a job within two days working in a factory packing store shelves and had what seemed to me like superhuman strength. I got promoted to line leader and built skids of shelves, bolts, backboards, plyboards, and long beams. The skids weighed from three hundred to over nine hundred pounds. I pushed them by myself down a one-person assembly line made from railroad ties and tracks that normally only men worked. There was a large pallet with wheels on the rails, and as I loaded the pallet with order parts, I had to push the skid down the line. After the miniature crane or forklift drivers hauled it off, I pushed the skid back to the beginning of the line and started the whole process all over again. I had been used to doing hard work, but not like that. When my children were smaller, I cleaned houses and offices as side work to help pay our bills because I had a hard time keeping a job due to my children having medical conditions. I went through babysitters and jobs like changing clothes.

By cleaning houses and offices, I didn't have to worry about not being able to keep a job. I could schedule my own hours, to a certain extent, and had regular clients I could depend on to keep their contracts. Word of mouth about me to their friends and coworkers led me to have too many request for me to fill. So, I decided to expand and draw up a five-year business plan to hire displaced homemakers who could pass a background and reference check to give them job training they could put on a resume. I wanted to file for a grant to help with buying vans, equipment, and insurance so that I could afford to hire people to work for me. I took my plan to several financial advisers to get different opinions, and they all told me it was a good plan and the only thing missing was the list of businesses in the area that were like my business, and a description of how my business compared to the other businesses, and why it would be good to invest in my business.

I was in the process of doing that when I had to face all those cancer recovery situations. I decided that since I was in better shape, I would start cleaning houses and offices again to supplement income, and to put references in my portfolio. I went back to work part-time cleaning for a doctor and his wife that I had cleaned for before I had cancer procedures done on me. He had been one of my children's doctors when they were little. One day he was home when I was cleaning for them and while he was walking around the island in their kitchen to get some more coffee, he asked me how many contracts I had built up since I had gone back to work. I told him just his because I was working in a factory twelve hours a day to pay the bills. He stopped in his tracks and said to me, "Virginia; I want you to find a different line of work. You may be in good shape now, but it won't last long, and you don't need to be doing that kind of work."

I promised him I would look into doing something different. After my son graduated high school I did just as I said I would do. One day after having my annual checkup with my Surgical Oncologist, I decided to go to the employment office to see what kind of work they had to offer. I was blessed because the lady that I saw said she knew of a place that she thought I would be perfect for. It was a major upscale department store. I had worked as a department manager in a local department store, but I knew nothing about fashion. I was in blue jeans all the time unless I was going to church. I did, however, know how to cater to people. I knew how to approach them, and how to read their body language, and how to make them feel special. She called the manager of the store and asked if the position was still available and told him who I was and that she was going to send me straight there to meet him.

Once there, we talked openly about my work history. I told him that I had never worked in an upscale environment, but I learned fast, and I loved to cater to people. I told him about my cleaning business and how I worked for catering companies cleaning up for them after wedding parties, and how I waited on the customers hand and foot to make them feel special. I told him that I knew I could do the same thing in that industry. I also told him I would study the product and wait on people while treating them the way they deserved to be treated so they could leave with a positive feeling. He hired me on the spot. I had to move back to Little Rock, but my children were older, and I was able to go where I needed to go to for work. I loved my new job. It was hard work, but nothing like pushing those skids down the assembly line. He had put me in one of the most messed up areas in the store. Ladies Accessories. I worked hard at learning and merchandising the products and greeting and waiting on the customers at the same time. It may sound strange to some people, but I truly loved assisting my customers. It made me feel like I was helping someone feel good who may have been having a hard time with something outside of that store. My customers seemed to enjoy my help, and even the owner's wife visited with me when visiting the store. I built up regular clients and became the new Credit Champion. I received gifts, awards, and bonus money every month for high sales of the promotions they were running.

Then my baby sister died. She had just found out three days before she died that she had liver cancer. She had caled me crying. It seemed impossible to me that she was gone. I had spoken to her the night before she died. She was sick, and had been having seizures. She had gone to the emergency room, and and they sent her home to go see her primary care doctor. She died during the night. We found out later that medicines she was taking interacted against each other causing her to have a seizure so bad it caused her to have a massive stroke. The medicines that interacted with each other were given to her by different doctors. Neither of them knew that she was on the other medicine and it caused her to die. It wasn't their fault. It wasn't her fault either. She had forgotten to tell the last doctor that changed her medicine that her other doctor she seen had also changed her medicine she got from him. Now days they have a medical network to prevent that from happening. I wish they had that then. If they had she may have still been alive today.

After my sister died my mother was afraid that she wasn't going see me again before she died, and she wanted me to move back home. The store manager asked me not to, and told me that if I needed to, I could take a couple of weeks off to spend with my mother so that she wouldn't feel so stressed. He told me that at the location closest to my mother I would never be able to meet my quota. My pay was high, and I had to meet a certain quota in order to keep my pay that high. He didn't think I could do it at the other location. However, as much as I loved my job there my mother came first. So, at my mother's request I made my move to the other location so that I could be closer to her, but I wasn't at my new work location very long before I realized that my old boss was right.

That store did not have the foot traffic the other store had that I had been working at, and it did not have the sales specialist position I specialized in because of the lack of sales in that location. However, I was able to promote the company credit card better than anyone else at the store because I told the clients how they could use the card as a discount card to save money instead of using it like a credit card. I had people thanking me all the time for telling them how to use it to save money. My customers were happy, the store manager was happy with it, and so was the credit department. The company was so impressed with my achievement for the store that they sent a representative of the credit department to find out how I got so many approved credit applications. I told him that I discouraged people from trying to sign up if they were certain that they would not pass a credit check because it would drop their credit score even lower than it already was, and I told them to wait at least six months without applying for any line of credit to apply for the card so that they would have a better chance of getting approved.

For the customers who was not concerned about not being able to pass a credit check, I told them that if they used their card they got approved for to pay for everything they had planned on paying cash with, that they could pay the bill off in full before the due date with the money they were going to spend anyway and would not owe anyone anything for their purchase. Instead they would be using the card like a rewards card to build points for discounts and free gifts. They said they were going to go back to corporate and teach their credit sales agents how I was doing it so that they could do it too. Everyone was happy as far as the credit situation was concerned. However, my quota could not be met, so I transferred to a different location about seventy-five miles away so that I would still be close to my mother and be in a better location to get my quota. After making that move things went straight downhill. I liked the area of my new location, and the people that I worked with, but I didn't have a car and had to take the city bus to work.

I had to leave my apartment three hours early to walk six blocks to a bus stop so that I could be at work on time. I was lucky that the bus service ran late so that on the days I had to work the evening shift I could still get a ride to my apartment before the city buses stopped running. However, on those days I would not get home until almost midnight and had to sometimes be up early the next morning to catch the six-a.m. bus. I stayed tired all the time from not getting enough sleep. I went to a local doctor to have my annual scans done, and they said I had something going on with my lungs. It could be scar tissue from when I had phenomena, or it could be an issue that needed to be dealt with concerning a relapse with cancer. I was told they needed to do more test. Those test also showed that I had something going on with my lungs. That would explain my feeling so tired.

Whatever it was it healed by itself, because when I went back the test were normal. There was some scar tissue left, but the spots they were concerned about were gone. I was relieved not only because I did not want to deal with cancer anymore, but also because I was having a hard time keeping my job. I was only at the new location for a couple of weeks when I had an accident and fractured my foot. My foot was in a lot of pain, but I could not take off work because I had to pay bills. My foot could not heal right because of the pressure of my being on it too much, and one day the bones in the top of my foot broke in half from the swelling causing too much pressure on my foot. When that happened I heard the snap, and the pain shooting to my brain was so bad that I thought I was going to be sick to my stomach. I couldn't stand on it at all. The doctor said that I could not do standup work anymore, and that ended that. I should have listened to my first manager. I loved my job but suddenly it was a thing of the past.

LIFE CHANGED AGAIN

I wound up moving back to where my mother, son, and daughters lived, and went to work as an assembly line worker in a factory making half the money I had gotten use to making for ten times harder work, and then later I got a job as a sales agent in a calling center. I unfortunately had a series of TIA's (Transient Ischemic Attack) that caused me to have stroke like symptoms that caused me to have short term memory problems. So, almost as soon as the idea would pop into my head as to what I could do to help me feel better I forgot about what I was thinking about doing. TIA's are not supposed to cause any permanent damage, however, I had what they called continuous TIAs, so I stayed confused and off balance most of the time. I believe the TIA's started from a blood clot I got in my foot after breaking my foot, and then getting a nasty spider bite. I wasn't using any type of home remedy at the time when I got the spider bite. I did not see the spider that had bitten me, and I seen no signs of any dangerous spiders being around me. So, I thought it would be okay with just putting rubbing alcohol and an antibiotic ointment on it. By the next day my ankle was swollen twice the size it should be, but instead of going to the doctor, like I should have done to begin with, I took an allergy pill and went to work.

That next day I had a blood clot that changed my life forever. I was in my bedroom sitting at my desk playing an online social media game with one of my other sisters. When suddenly I had a severe pain in my foot and then it shot up my left leg. I thought I had a leg cramp and changed position.Then I heard a loud sound like a cross between a door slamming and a gun going off inside of my head. I saw a bright white light, then a feeling like someone had thrown me into my body and across the room. I crawled on the floor dazed and not able to see, and it felt like my heart was constantly fluttering. Not beating. Just fluttering. I tried to call out for help, but I couldn't talk. I don't know how long I was like that before my son-in-law found me and helped me get an ambulance. By the time the ambulance arrived my heart was beating again, but not normal, and I had blurry vision.

I was treated in the emergency room, diagnosed as having a TIA, and then released. The next day I had one even worse that left me with continuous TIAs and waiting for a major stroke that thankfully never happened. However, for about four months I had continuous TIAs and couldn't walk at all without assistance. I would bounce off the walls as if though I was drunk. My doctors ran a series of test on me, and seen that I had extra activity going on with my blood work that had not been there at a previous visit, and they made an appointment for me to go to Little Rock to see a cancer specialist to be evaluated for a recurrence of cancer. Before I left the clinic that day a Chaplin visited with me to make sure I was ready to meet my maker. My caseworker at the doctor's clinic told me she had arranged for me to stay in Little Rock at a special kind of shelter for people who could work full time so that they could save their money and learn to be financially independent. They had programs to help people with getting good employment and how to achieve their financial goals. In some situations, they would make an exception and take someone in that could not work full time. I was one of those exceptions.

The shelter knew of my medical conditions and had agreed to let me stay as long as I could work part time if I had to have cancer treatments. If I could not work part time, they would try to help me find a place to stay. I went to Little Rock a few days before my doctor's appointment to check into the shelter and so as to participate in a breast cancer awareness event. I walked the full race distance in that event. I nearly passed out walking across the bridge while talking to my mother on the cell phone. I told her I was going to finish that race even if it killed me. She told me that if I didn't take it easy it just might kill me. She convinced me to sit down for a few minutes before finishing the race. I did as she asked, but after drinking some water I was right back up within a few minutes. I weaved to the left, and other walkers helped me across the hill on the bridge. I went on to finish the race. I wasn't the first one to cross the finish line, but I finished it just like I was determined to do.

The next day I paid for my hardheaded behavior. After eating breakfast, I went outside of where I was staying to sit at a picnic table and to call my mother, son, and daughters. As I got up to go back inside, I had another TIA so bad that it blinded me. Just like a certain medication does that I had tried. I could not tell if I was standing right side up or if I was standing on my head. I had absolutely no since of direction at all and fell on the ground. Some people standing close to where I was ran to help me up, and when they saw that I could not see they called for an ambulance. When the ambulance arrived, I could see some images, but I still could not make out anything. It was a couple of hours before I got my sight back, and when I did get my vision back it was like looking through two different windows at the same time.

They had the same picture, but one looked small and was inside of the other picture. Like a picture frame inside of a picture frame, and they both were shaking like an earthquake was going on inside of my head. I was hospitalized for several days, and I had to have physical therapy to learn how to walk and brush my teeth again. For several years after that I suffered what seemed like permanent vertigo and short-term memory problems, among other things. I had constant anxiety because I could not get my balance, and I felt like I was falling even when I was sitting down.

They tried to give me medication for the vertigo, but my body rejected it and made my blood pressure drop too low. I just wanted to be still so that I wouldn't feel like I was falling, but even that did not help, and I couldn't just stay sitting down. I was still alive, and I had to do what I had to do to stay alive. The TIA's themselves did not hurt. Or, if it did, I could not remember it hurting. What hurt was trying to force my body to remember to breath, to walk straight afterwards without falling towards my left and busting my shins or knees open, and trying to stay calm because of my feeling like I was falling all the time. I did not have a stroke, but something going on in my neck and head was causing me to have constant TIAs.

I had swollen lymph nodes in my neck causing restrictions on my arteries, and I had calcifications on my brain stem that may have been a contributing factor in my illness and needed further workup. To this day I can honestly tell you that the hardest part of having those TIA's was surviving them. I had to learn how to control the anxiety, and to remember to write in my journals to help me remember and keep up with my activity and things I needed to do. To make things even worse I am also allergic to iodine, so they could not run the needed test to find out just what was causing the problem. So, I just had to deal with it the best I could. I had to stay positive and focus on God being there to help me through it. A few times I had severe symptoms with my brain not telling my heart to beat right or forgetting to tell me to breath when I was supposed to. Sometimes my body reacts the opposite of what it is supposed too.

One day I was so calm that a doctor told me that I should have been having severe anxiety even worse than what I was having. My heart was beating off pattern, not just beating fast, but I was calm like nothing was wrong with me. The doctor thought their machines were not working properly, so they changed the machine they had me connected to. It gave the same reading. He told me that I was different than anyone he had ever treated. There was a few other doctors who said I was different too. The doctors said I was a complicated case. I knew they were wright when they said that to me, but instead of responding like I should have done and talked to them about it, I stayed quiet waiting for them to continue with why they thought I was different. There was one special doctor who said that to me, and I wanted to say something in response, but I was afraid that someone would think I was crazy. I was wrong for that because I knew I was different than some people. I should have said, "Your different too." He was different. He had the glow of life in him, and when I seen the Spirit of God shining in him I had enough faith in God to not give up. As soon as he touched me I felt a surge of electricity go through me. I knew I was going to be okay. But being different did not make recovering any easier. Just because I wasn't dead yet, like they said most people with my conditions would have been, that did not mean that I was doing okay.

It was a constant battle and struggle to maintain myself. I had a hard time trying to remember to do the things I needed to do for my basic survival needs. If it wasn't for God putting the right people in my path I may not have made it as well as I had. Some doctors, and insurance companies, say that is a reason not to help stroke and heart attack victims. I was told that stroke and heart attack patients lead poor quality lives if they survive, and that they cause family and or financial burden from not being able to take care of themselves. I understand that it could take a toll on the patients' families and that the road to recovery is costly, but I believe that families should stick together and help one another. However, some people claim the burden isn't worth the fight. They don't take into consideration that the person might want to take that chance and that it would be worth the uphill fight to stay alive. Once the patient heals or gets better it's all just a memory. Just like the pain from having a baby. You remember you went through the pain and that it hurt, but after you have the baby you don't feel the pain any longer. And just like everything else that we survive in life, it makes life more meaningful than what it was before you went through whatever it was that caused so much pain. As for me, I did not give up because I could remember my grandma saying telling me, "This too shall pass." All I had to do was pray and believe like my uncle talked about, do what I was medically told to do that wouldn't harm me, and wait.

For a couple of weeks after I had gotten out of the hospital both the residents and the employees of the shelter help to take care of me while I recovered. The employees monitored my medicine and took my food to me, the residents helped me to the restroom, and stood by the shower door to make sure I did not fall. There was only a few who was not friendly and helpful, but I did not take it personally because they were not friendly to anyone. However, one day one of them seen I was a little off balance and she ran to catch me to keep me from falling. God was with me after having the TIA's too , because not only did the people at the shelter help take care of me, I recovered well enough to get a full-time job at a good company. That was how I met my future husband. Not at the company, instead it was at the shelter. He would help me get to and from the bus stop so that I could look for a job.

After working for about a month, my boss in Northeast Arkansas found out through my family that I was back working and called asking me to go back to work. Evidently, they liked my work too. I was grateful that my father had taught me to enjoy my work, and to do my best at everything I done. Rather I liked it or not I needed to do the right thing because it was the right thing to do. He taught me about job integrity, and it had paid off in a lot of ways. I told the people at the shelter, and my new friend, about my boss wanting me to go back to work for her. I totally dismissed seeing the doctors that I had been sent there to see. For some reason I forgot about them. My new friend reminded me of my doctor appointment I had told him about and nearly begged me to stay there. He wanted us to live together. I did not want to shack-up. So, he asked me to marry him. I wasn't thinking straight when I said yes. It was too soon after my having that bad TIA, and I did not know him that well at all.

But I figured that other people have married people that they were arranged to be married to, or married people they met overseas, and most of those marriages worked because they wanted it to. I was supposed to be dying. I did not want to die alone, and I did not want to shack up. He was willing to be there with me unlike my ex, so I married him. Just like that it was done. When my children and other family members found out about it, they were upset. They were afraid that my new friend was taking advantage of me. They never talked hateful or disrespectful to him, but they tried to get me to leave him and stay at the shelter. They did not offer for me to go stay with them though. Even the people at the shelter tried to talk me out of moving in with him. I thought he was Heaven sent and I chose to stay with him, but it did not last long.

THE FIGHT OF MY LIFE

We argued all of the time, and it stressed me out too much and made my blood pressure go high. I wound up in the hospital from a blood clot and a mass in my left leg and decided that I needed to change my environment. Later, we became friends, but at that time we were too different, and I was too sick, for us to work things out. So, one day after we had an argument I left. It wasn't until after I left that I realized that I did not have anywhere to go. By that time my son had joined the military, by eldest daughter was married to someone who did not want to take care of me, and my youngest daughter was living with her boyfriend and his family. I knew that my sister would only let me stay for a couple of weeks.

The only people I really knew was people who I worked with, who I was not related to, and who I did not want to burden with my problems. I didn't have a church family anymore because I had gotten out of going to church when a pastor at a church I went to for years told me the day before my daughter's doctor appointment three hours away to tell me that he didn't think it was right for the church to help me because it was enabling me to be single. My transmission was slipping, and I was afraid of driving it that far away from home for fear of breaking down on the highway with three children with me. I had asked him to ask the people who usually drive people to their doctor's appointments it they could take me if I paid them for their time and gas. I asked him three weeks in advance, but he waited until the day before my daughter's appointment to tell me that. It wasn't my fault that my children and I were alone.

I was so hurt that I stopped going to church on a regular basis, but I never stopped praying or praising God. I figure that pentecostal churches would not accept me because I was divorced. So why go to church? I should not have let evil forces use that man to drive me away from church and the people who loved me in the church, and who I loved. I should not have let his determination to make me get back with my children's father, who by that time was married to someone else, divert me from praising God with other believers. By doing so, I not only lost the praise and worship I shared with others, I lost my church family and support. Because of that my daughter missed her much needed appointment. I had to take her to a local doctor to evaluate her for the specialist. Because of my leaving the church there was no one for there for me when my children were little, and there was no one there to help me then either.

So, I called the shelters and they were full. A nice lady at one of the shelters was helpful and called the surrounding counties to see if they had a bed open. There was no luck. So, they called the St. Louis homeless network to see if they had beds available because that was where I was from. They did and they gave me twenty-four hours to check in. The lady at the shelter in Little Rock bought me a bus ticket to St. Louis and took me to the bus station. I was on my way to the place I was born but knew very little about. Normally I only went there to visit family. It had been years since I had been back, but I knew my family there would not turn their back on me because that just wasn't what families done. The problem with that is that when I got there I could not get hold of them. They had moved after my grandfather and step-grandmother had died, and I had no way of knowing where to find them. So, I had to stay in the shelter anyway.

At first I was ashamed of it, but it didn't take long for me to appreciate being able to be at the shelter because it helped me. Staying in a shelter made me feel on alert, and that helped me to stay focused on what was going on around me. I also was grateful to be off the streets and for the people at the shelter. They helped me get the resources that I needed to survive. Resources like medical insurance, food, city bus passes, and getting me help to see a doctor who could get me linked up with any specialist that I may have needed at the time. But the shelter was closed during the day, and I had to leave and go out into the world with very little balance from the vertigo I was having, and with no money. I was barely functional at the time. However, my instincts led me to go to the library to learn natural ways of healing. I could have wondered around that big city with no direction at all, but with the help of strangers I was able to find my way to the library.

I had always heard that homeless people hung out at libraries and I didn't want to be like that. But there I was seeking refuge from the city and weather in the most common place anyone could go. Other than having a place to get off the street, the library served as a greatly needed tool for my getting better. It was there that I done research on some of the natural remedies I learn about from my grandmother when I was a child and when she and I were both going through cancer together. The kindness of the librarian who help me with the computer put me in the position for my instincts to kick in at the right time in the right place. After having a crying episode from not remembering how to type, and after the librarian helped me with a typing tool, I instinctively researched the things planted in my memory by my grandmother.

I could not remember much, but I knew what to look up. Both of my grandmother's taught against sugar. So, I researched cancer and sugar. What I learned was that cancer feeds off sugar. Some cancers use our hormones as food too. As mine was. By doing so it threw my system out of whack. Some days I didn't know if I was standing up or laying down. Literally. I would feel like I was falling while setting down. Even scarier was the times I would stop breathing for no reason, and then I would suddenly gasp for air. It was like having bad sleep apnea spells while being wide awake. My brain would forget to tell my body to breath. Sort of like walking dead. I could barely remember my grandmother teaching me about the natural remedies she used, but somehow my instincts kicked in and led me to want to know more. I had bad reactions to a lot of the medicines the doctors tried me on, and I was afraid to try any more medicines for fear of having another bad reaction like I had before. I knew that if I was going to survive, I was going to have to stay positive, and I would need to use some of those old-fashioned remedies to help me with the side effects I was having so that I could take care of myself and keep my strength up so that my body could fight off whatever was going on inside of it. Between the vertigo, staying confused, fatigue, having dizzy spells, and staying nauseous most of the time, I spent my every waking hour fighting off symptoms and side effects of the medicines my new doctors were trying me on, and or from the illnesses I was trying to recover from.

In my desperation of trying to figure out just what was wrong with me I accidently made a few people angry at me over my questioning them as to why the test results from procedures they had performed on me did not show or have the results from what they was supposed to be testing me for. I meant no disrespect, but out of frustration from not being able to get test results I accused a radiologist of purposely leaving out the information. I thought they sliced out what they were supposed to be looking at because a radiologist technician told me the image had been sliced when I asked why the test results said noting about the area that was supposed to have been tested. For that, I am truly sorry. Little did I know at that time that one of my extended family members, who I had reconnected with and who went to a doctor's appointment with me, felt the need to tell the doctors that they didn't think I could deal with knowing about whatever was going on with me.

Excuse me, but I was not in a coma. I was not so sick that I could not understand what people were saying to me, so why did they go to my extended family to talk about my issues? What about the privacy act they were supposed to be upholding? I was the one trying to survive whatever was going on in my body. I was the one taking care of myself, no one was doing it for me. No one except the people in the shelters even tried to help me, but people waisted no time telling me how I was an embarrassment to them. They insulted me for staying in a shelter and told me that I should get a job so that I could do better for myself. Now these are people who offered to let me go stay with them, and in return I helped a little with cleaning their house because she couldn't do it anymore. There were some days I was so off balance I couldn't do it either. But they thought I should get a job. Hello out there! What world did they come from?

What made them think I could keep a full-time job that I would have to have in order to rent my own place. Some days I could barely stand up on my own. I wasn't mad at my family for not wanting to help me. After all, what people do with their time and money is up to them, but please, there was no reason to belittle me because I needed help. Everything was fine until one day she walked down to the basement where I stayed at in a little apartment they had made for their son, and caught her husband peeping in the bathroom when I was taking a shower. I didn't know what was going on. All I heard was a bunch of screaming. I jumped out of the shower and grabbed a towel and ran to see what was wrong, but all I seen was the backs of them going up the steps. I got dressed and went up to ask what was wrong and she asked me to go back downstairs she would talk to me later. I did as I was asked. Later she came down the steps and told me that I was going to have to start looking for another place to stay and told me what happened.

She told me she wasn't mad at me, and that she had people tell her in the past that he had tried to get them to be with him. She said she was sorry, but I couldn't stay there after that happened. The story of my life. Someone always saying they were sorry for something and walking away. I was the one put out. Not him.

That hurt. I loved her. We had been close when we were younger. I finally found out how to get hold of her, and everything was good until he pulled that mess. I sometimes believe he did it on purpose because he talked hateful to her when he thought no one was looking, and he may have done that, or made it look like he was doing that, just so she would make me leave so she wouldn't have anyone around to help her. But, only him and God knows the truth. That night at dinner time he told me that I shouldn't have any problems finding a job and getting my own place.

He said that they would take me back to the shelter the next day, and that it was going to be embarrassing if people at church found out I was staying at a shelter. He told me I needed to get a job so I could do better for myself. He was so heartless. Calm. It felt like he did that on purpose, and I said so. Later that night it stormed real bad, and tornados went through the area. The storm made to local river flood so bad that it flooded my downstairs apartment. I took pictures of the water running down the walls from the basement windows. Even if he had not done that I still would have had to move. If it wasn't for the basement flooding I would not have been able to stay at the shelter either. Strange how something good can come out of something so bad.

As for her meddling in my affairs, I guess between our dinner conversation and her being upset over her husband being caught, by her, peeking in the bathroom while I was taking a shower it led her to take it out on me and cause un-necessary strife in my life that effected my medical care. Something I never would have thought of happening happened. I never would have found out about the doctors not wanting me to know about my medical condition if it wasn't for the fact that at the time I had filed for disability and had to go to court. While in court the Judge asked a doctor if she had gone over all of my medical records, and if she had did she think that I was disabled, and if she thought I was disabled how long did she believe that I would be disabled. The doctor replied that she "believed me to be disable because of ..." and gave a list of codes. Then she told the Judge that she could not say how long I would be disabled because, "most patients with her medical conditions usually expire within six months, and she has well over exceeded that time period."

My attorney looked at me and smiled and gave me a thumbs up! That's right. A thumbs up! I looked at him wondering if he understood what she said. How could that be good news? Of course, to him it was great news. It meant a paycheck, but for me it was a death sentence. I looked up at the Judge with the thought in my head, "Did you see that?" He must have read my mind, because he shrugged his shoulders and tilted his head with a strange look on his face as if to say, "Oh well, that's how he gets his money." I broke down crying. The Judge asked me why I was crying because it was over. That meant that I won. I told him that the doctors I was going to told me there was nothing seriously wrong with me and that I didn't have cancer anymore. I assumed she was talking about cancer. My attorney changed the subject, and the Judge went on to be formal and dismissed court.

When I went to the doctor a few days later I decided to test him. I wanted to know if he knew what the court knew. It was the same old stuff when I went in. Just a checkup. I am assuming since they thought I was dying but not doing anything to prevent it; the appointments that they kept making for me probably were just to make sure that I was still alive, and then they would dismiss me. When I asked him about my blood test that day, he told me that my red blood cells were three times what they were supposed to be again. I asked what was causing it and I just what I had. He made off like I just had continuous TIA's and tried to dismiss it. I asked him why I was having them, and he changed the subject telling me about when he wanted me to return.

As he was leaving the room, I asked him to wait, and told him about my going to court, and what they said. He just sat there. He did not say one word for about a minute. Then he told me he had to see the next patient and that he was sorry that I had to go through that. He walked out of the door leaving me to sit there alone wondering why everything was such a big secret. What could possibly be so bad that it was too bad to tell me? Was something being covered up to cover up someone's mistake, or was I part of some kind of experiment that I didn't know anything about? If that's the case, shouldn't I give approval first? There had to be some reason why they didn't want me to know what was going on with me. Other people who were dying knew they were dying and what they were dying from, they had the chance to fight for their life, or to prepare to dye. Why couldn't I have the same rights they had?

When I checked out, I asked for a summary of my visit showing my medical condition. The receptionist was a young and inexperienced lady who was filling in for the normal receptionist. She told me she couldn't give me a printout of my doctor visit summary because it said I wasn't allowed to be given any information. I questioned her as to why and told her that I always get a summary. She turned the computer monitor screen towards me so that I could see the bright red words on the black screen saying that for my safety medical information was not to be disclosed to "THE PATIENT." Hello, that was me it was talking about. I was the patient it was referring to. It was my body. Why was I not allowed to know what was going on with my own body? That seemed illegal to me. I could be walking too much and fall from the sidewalk and fall out in front of traffic and cause an accident, and cause someone to get hurt bad or killed because they would not let me be a part of my own team and know what was going on with me and what to do or not to do.

I wanted to know why, and all I could find out was that my family had told my doctor that I was not mentally stable enough to be able to deal with any serious news. Wow! How easy was it for a jealous family member to pretend to want to take me to the doctor just to stab me in the back, and the doctors let her do it. She wasn't even on my list of family members to notify about emergencies. How could they do that without even questioning me about it. I cannot begin to tell you the pain and distrust it caused me to have towards the doctors I was using at the time. I had already had to deal with two doctors who did not want to treat me for cancer. One who refused to do test on me to see if I had breast cancer because he thought I was too young to have breast cancer; even though I had the symptoms and a strong family history of having different types of cancer. And one doctor who refused to do test on me because he said it was too late in the game.

I remembered back when my husband and I were waiting to see him. A resident doctor had been in my room several times questioning me and told my husband and I that he agreed with my doctors who referred me there, and that he needed to run everything past his supervisor and would be back to talk to me. He came back and told us that his supervisor agreed, and that they were going to run some test of their own to make sure of what we were dealing with so that "WE" could come up with a treatment plan. He told me that he was going to put the orders in, and that his supervisor would be in to talk to me about it. My husband had been trying to cheer me up by tickling me and kissing around on my face and neck. I was trying to get him to stop, and then I saw that doctor walk through the door. He took one look at my husband kissing me on the side of my face and tickling my side and made what I called a rat eye look.

His eyes widened and then narrowed so much they almost squinted. He asked me why I was there, and I told him that I had been referred to him by my doctors to be reevaluated for a cancer recurrence. He straight up told me in front of my husband, "It is too late in the game to be doing test like that. If you wanted to be treated for it, you should have done that in the beginning." I could not believe my ears. I thought I must have misunderstood him because the resident said that his supervisor had agreed that I needed testing to be reevaluated. So, I tried to explain why my other doctors wanted him to reevaluate me. He said that he wasn't going to have a twenty-five-hundred-dollar test done on me for something that I should have had done in the beginning. I asked, "How are you going to reevaluate me if you don't run test on me?" He told me I needed to return to the doctor who sent me there to find out what I needed to know. Then he walked out of the room leaving my husband and I to stare at each other in disbelief. I had to go through channels to request another appointment to see a different doctor. That doctor's supervisor told us that we must have misunderstood the resident, and if not then he apologized for the student resident doctor misunderstanding his supervisor. They done blood work on me and said I was normal. Nothing was wrong with me. Nothing at all. He was like dealing with the doctor who thought I was too young to have breast cancer. I wish the other doctors had help me go back to my original oncologist whom I loved, but I had lost my insurance, and I was at the mercy of the program that was funding my visit there and had to use the doctor they said I had to go to, but that doctor was like the doctor who refused to do a mammogram on me. He wasn't going to budge.

I never could figure out why that man got so mad. Was he having a bad day, did he have me confused with another patient who had the same name? As it turned out there was several patients who went to that clinic with my name. I thought to myself that was a possibility because I had to take my payment receipt to the billing office so that they could credit my account because they had applied my copayment to the wrong account with the same name. I couldn't help to wonder if he was caught off guard when he walked in the door and seen my husband trying to kiss on me? His eyes getting wide and then narrowing told me that even though I hoped that was not the case, he may have felt disrespected, and it may have played a part in the scenario. I meant no disrespect, and I am sure that my husband didn't either. He was trying to cheer me up.

He wasn't the only one I accidently offended. My fighting against the orders to not disclose my medical information to me is what led up to my making a couple of "in-the-know" people mad at me and it trickled down the line causing people to have opinions about me who should not have an opinion about me at all. I know this because even my eye doctor told me that she had heard of me, but she couldn't remember what it was about. Why were they talking about me to an eye doctor? Who was talking about me to my eye doctor? Why was my name out there at all? My information should only be between the doctors who treated me and the people who played a part in my recovery. It should not be thrown out there like entertainment, or for a gossip session. My case should only be discussed at work, not in the breakroom, country clubs, restrooms, women's meetings, men's meetings, taxicabs, elevators, carpools, or anyplace else besides where they officially made their medical decisions for patients. It led me to wonder if someone was trying to cover their tracks.

I know it sounds paranoid, but it happens, and look at what I had been through. I would have to be brain dead not to realize that my name should not have been out there like that. If someone was trying to cover their track what was it they were trying to cover up? Do the other doctors know, and are they trying to help cover something up? Or are they being used to deny me medical care? I felt helpless and turned to God's mercy to saving me. Here I was in a different city, and I still could not get anything done. When I first got there, doors opened for me on all levels. I got a new primary care doctor, new oncologist, food resources, shelter, city bus fare, and eyeglasses. I had a sleep study done on me and found out that I had sleep apnea and had to use a C-Pap machine to sleep with. I was always afraid that someone in the shelter was going to steal it because I had nowhere to store it.

It seemed as though I met the perfect people in every direction I turned. There was one lady at one of the shelters who I believe was, and I'm sure she still is, an exceptional person. I had a lot of pressure on my right ear, and it was swollen all the time. It would hurt all the way down into my neck. This lady was and Egyptian who still used ancient remedies too. I had an ear ache and she told me about an ancient remedy for ear accumulation and pain. It works. I cannot share it on here due to her not giving me permission to do so, but you won't believe the difference it makes. To get back on to the point I was making is that doctors, nurses, and everyone in my medical care circle was nice to me and behaved like they cared. Then they got my medical records transferred to them and questioned me about why I seen a different oncologist in an accusing way like I was purposely going to different places to get a different answer. I tried to explain about my losing my insurance and having to go through a program who sent me to a doctor in their network.

I told them that nothing came of it because that doctor did not agree with the other doctors. Everything stopped again. Everything except my primary care doctor, dentist, and my new gynecologist. I was blessed to have a good dentist that was in the same clinic as my primary care doctor. She was awesome. My broken off teeth were hurting me so bad that I could not sleep or eat. I was scared of going back to a dentist because the two dentist I had gone to within the last few years were terrible. When they pulled a tooth, they nearly lifted me out of the chair pulling on me. I was afraid one of them was going to break my jaw. The other one of actually put his knee in my stomach and was holding me down in the chair with his knee while he jerked the tooth out of my head. I thought he was going to break my neck. I hurt everywhere after that.

They both left broken pieces of tooth in my mouth, and for months I would have sharp fragments working their way through my gums. Every time I bit down on something, I had sharp shooting pains that felt like someone was stabbing me in my mouth. This dentist was different. She was able to pull several teeth at one time without hurting me or jerking on me. She would wiggle the needle into my gums which kept the injection from hurting. She also used adrenaline in my gums instead of the normal numbing medicine that I always broke out with. She was nice and calmly talked to me the entire time she worked on me. I couldn't answer anything besides uhhu or huuh for yes or no. She didn't talk about her personal life to her assistant like I wasn't there like the other dentist did. She would have several teeth out within just a few minutes, and when the medicines wore off, I didn't hurt half as bad as what I did after seeing the other Dentist. She only had one tooth to break on her, and she vacuumed it out so as not to leave any broken pieces to work themselves out. She cared.

The gynecologist was also at the same clinic my primary doctor was at. She was a very nice lady who also believed that I needed the cancer treatment that I could not take because I wasn't menopausal. She said that by having a hysterectomy I not only would be getting rid of the fibroid tumors. I would be able to take the other cancer treatment to help keep the cancer from coming back. My monthly cycles were getting worse because of the tumors, so my gynecologist decided that if I agreed she could clamp my uterus shut so that I would not be bleeding so bad, and that it would force my body to start going into menopause. She told me that it was important that I understood that I had to keep my scheduled appointment to have the hysterectomy she had scheduled for me because the plastic clamp she was putting in me had to be removed within two weeks or it would cause inflammation.

Well, I became homeless and was staying in a shelter, and the shelter would not let me stay there if I had the surgery because it closed down during the day, so the surgery kept getting put off. It wasn't her fault that I ran out of time at the shelter or that my family member I was staying with when she scheduled the surgery said that I couldn't stay there anymore because of her husband and that it left me with nowhere to stay to recover from the surgery. She tried to help me, and I am grateful to her for trying because she cared too. Even after I moved back to Arkansas, I still could not get the surgery done because the first doctor who was going to do my surgery had already been paid to do it and no one else in Arkansas could get paid to do the surgery unless she paid for it to be done.

When I tried to get back in contact with that doctor nobody had heard of me. I was not in the records, and the doctor was no longer there. I could only assume that she wasn't able to go back to work like they thought she could, and they took her patients records with her belongings. That's sad, but how do I get hold of her to see if the billing company she used at the time returned the payment, or if they kept it for her? No one would help me find out. I guess they was afraid I was going to try to sue someone. That was the furthest thing from my mind. I just wanted the surgery. So, I still have not had that surgery, and I still have that clamp wrapped around my uterus opening. I am not a doctor, but I am sure that skin has grown around that clamp. I believe that clamp and all the other plastic in my body is why I have so much inflammation, and why I have to fight so hard with trying to keep the inflammation down. Before moving back to Arkansas my oncologist referred me to see a psychiatrist because my family was "concerned" about my welfare. Everything went downhill again. The psychiatrist wanted me to try a different anxiety medication even though I had told him about my having a lot of allergies and reverse reactions to a lot of medicines related to the medicine he wanted me to try. He wouldn't listen to me. He talked to me like he thought I was refusing because I just wanted to stay on what I was taking. Well, yes that was true, but so was my allergies.

So, I agreed to try it, but within less than twenty-four hours I was in the emergency room. That is when my heart was beating on a different pattern than what it was supposed to be beating on, and the doctor in the emergency room told me that I should have been having severe anxiety. Instead I was calm. I was at peace. The exact opposite of what I should have been feeling. I don't know if it was because that medicine was working the opposite on me, or if it was because of the mess going on in my brain. When I should have been at peace, I was having anxiety. I couldn't take most medicines for it, and the psychiatrist did not want me to take what had been working for me because he thought I should be on one of the newer medicines. So, I had to find something else to help ease my symptoms. When I was doing research for natural remedies, I tried to find natural resources for anxiety too.

I found a few, like eating turkey in the evening to help you rest, but nothing like the medicine that I had been taking that worked good for me. I had to stay focused on God. God was all I had. As I got sicker my belief that I was going to be okay bewildered people. Especially the psychiatrist. I guess he tried to convince me there was no God, or he was wondering what I thought about God not saving me yet because he asked me, "If God was going to save you why hasn't he already done it?" He thought I was delusional for believing that God must have been letting me get that sick before healing me so that others, and myself, could see that miracles still exist, either that or it just wasn't my time to die yet. As delusional as it sounded at the time to him or anyone else, they cannot deny the fact that I am still alive and kicking. If I gave into what they believed I would have been long gone. I think that is why a lot of people give up. They are told they have no hope to live, and or they make people feel like they are not worth trying to save. You can be honest with someone about their condition without making them feel worthless or a waist of time. As it turned out he was the doctor who put the order in the system not to let me know about my conditions. I tried to give him the benefit of doubt, and decided to test him to see if he would be honest with me by agreeing to go along with something he said just to let him know afterwards that the receptionist showed me the computer monitor and that I saw what it said about not letting me know about my medical conditions.

I told him that I didn't know why he would put that in the system without talking to me first, but it made me feel like I couldn't trust him to be on my team. I also told him that I wanted a doctor who would let me know what was going on with my body. It was my body he was being paid to take care of, and if anyone had any right to know what was wrong with me, it was me. After all, how was I to know what to do or not to do in relation to my condition if I didn't know what my condition was? If it happened to him, he would want to know too. I never went back to see him again. There was no reason to go back because I couldn't trust him to tell me the truth. As far as I know he never did remove that tag on me he put in the system.

I know it doesn't sound very Christian of me, but I would take my extended family member to court and sue her for interfering with my medical care if I thought for sure that she had purposely tried to keep me from getting the help that I needed. I have to give her the benefit of doubt in thinking she probably said that because she herself would not have wanted to know what was going on if she personally had to face a life threating illness. But I am not her and she is not me. To this day I do not know what it is that the doctor in court was referring to. It is in my profile in the "Medical Network" that doctors and insurance companies use to keep up with a person's medical visits and treatments at different locations so that they are all on the same team with a patient's health care. The problem with that is that they all thought I was delusional, and that I was too mentally ill to know my own condition. I guess they thought I was too weak minded or fragile to know what was wrong with me and would go crazy or something.

Or maybe they thought I was too brain dead to realize I was sick, and that they were no longer helping me like they were before I got that label stuck to my name. I got the impression that not one of them cared enough to question if I was that ill, or if I had been that ill if my mental state had changed. I guess to them I was a lost cause. All I know is that even before that happened several times in the past, I had been told that I wouldn't live long due to an enzyme disease causing my body not to break down glycerin. What that condition is called I do not know, and if it is related to what the doctor in the court room said I was dying from I do not know that either. It looked like God was all I had and could trust. Now I try to avoid doctors at all cost because I feel there is no point in my going if they aren't going to help me. When that happens, I have to fight off depression because it is demeaning and causes me to feel like they think I am not good enough for someone to try to save.

But I break down and go every few months because my insurance requires it, and because I cannot get natural remedies for asthma attacks, severe emergencies, or for TIA's when I do have them. So, I have to go in. But my faith in them has changed from what it used to be. Now when I go to the doctor I go with the question in the back of my mind of rather or not I'm going to have a caring doctor who I can trust to let me know what is going on with me and help me fix it, or at least help me understand what is going on with my body, and what to expect or look out for and who will let me be a part of my recovery. Or am I going to get a doctor who is going to look on their black screen and see those red words not to share my medical information with me because I am delusional and cannot be trusted to know the truth about myself, and then dance around my questions and treat me like I am crazy or leave me set without any answers as they walk out of the door like it's not their problem to help me?

In my opinion there should be a law against doctors who get paid to take care of people, but don't let the patient know what is wrong with them or who doesn't even try to solve what is causing their symptoms. Just treating some of the symptoms without trying to take care of what is causing the symptoms is like paying a roofer to put a new roof on your house, but all they do is slap a patch on it to cover it up so you can't see the problem until a squirrel falls through your roof. Wouldn't you want your money back or expect him to have to pay the insurance company back for services not rendered? It seems like it is the same thing to me; only worse because it is our bodies they are getting paid to fix, but instead some of them are jacking us around like shade tree mechanics coning people who don't know anything about how to work on cars so that they can keep you coming back to milk the insurance companies and make more money. That's scary. I'm glad that most of them are not like that.

Or like the Public Defender (Protector?) who gets paid five hundred dollars by the state for losing a case they are supposed to be defending, but they only get paid three hundred dollars for winning. Seems backwards to me, especially when you sit in court and it is obvious that some of them do not even try to get the defendant cleared. In some cases, they cause the defendant to get a worse sentence than what they would have gotten without their help. The Public Defender has to swap up every so often from representing the Public Defender's Office to working on the Prosecutor's team. It makes you wonder if they ever really switch sides to begin with. I can't really blame the doctors or the attorneys because it is the fault of how the system for the insurance companies, and the legal system was set up. They were trying to minimize spending and time so they could treat people like an assembly line. Move them in, move them out. The faster they moved them through the process with as little cost as possible the more money they made. It's just how business works. But we are people, not product on an assembly line, and we have living souls, and we deserve the right to have proper medical care. So, to me withholding medical care from someone is the same thing as playing a part in causing someone's death.

They say not to try to save someone who they think is dying. Why? Just because they think they are dying that doesn't mean that they will. And if the illness or injury is so bad that it is almost for certain they are going to dye there is no reason to treat a dying person like they are not worth trying to save. It's bad enough they have to die before they are ready to, why add hurtful insult on top of fear and injury? That's treating someone like they have no regard for their life. In courts prosecutors always stress how someone has little to no regard for someone's life that in on trial. Why doesn't the same thing apply in medical care? Can you imagine how a dying person feels knowing they are not good enough to save? Why doesn't that matter? It matters for dog, whales, gorillas, monkeys, cats, birds, and even snakes. We try to save them when they get hurt or bad sick. People get charged for neglect if they don't get their pet proper medical care when it's needed. I am not downplaying the need to save animals, but when did the feelings, lives, and the souls of whales and other animals become any more important than the value of the lives of people?

Is the life of a human not worth any more than a sick or injured horse? Are we being put out of our misery?

Here's some questions. Does it have anything to do with rather or not they are afraid the bill won't get paid if the patient dies, and what about if someone is an organ donor? I ask this because years ago I watched a boy die in a hospital in Southeast Missouri who was in the unit directly across where my family was. That teenager had a driver's license that said he was a donor. The mother was begging them to help her son. They told her by law they couldn't because he was an organ donor. She started screaming and refused to let them touch her son after they said that. They called the police on her. I felt like the police should have been called on the hospital.

The police did not arrest her, but they got her to calm down, then she collapsed. They had to work on her. I don't know how it turned out. Later a lady who worked at the revenue department and I were talking about my being an organ donor, and I told her to remove it from my driver's license, and why. She said she seen parents in there all the time talking their children into being an organ donor and how she felt like it was wrong for that very reason. Donating your organs after they tried to save you but couldn't is one thing, but not trying to save you at all because you are an organ donor is something totally different. They don't tell you that when you sign up to be an organ donor. Shameful.

It is also shameful that some people abuse their power and negligently with just the press of a finger write life changing instructions in a national data base that could cause people from getting the care they need. I bet they would not like it if it happened to them. Wow. I never seen that one coming. I have never purposely done anything to anyone to hurt them, so I never could have seen this kind of treatment coming towards me. To me denying me medical care that I need is the same things a playing a part in my death. To me I believe it's no different than someone going out in the street to kill someone. Like I said before, in a court room a judge would look down on someone who has no regard for someone else's life. Something to think about. So, what did I do? I prayed. I still pray. I try not to let it steal my joy in life and make me too depressed over some doctors acting like they don't care about what happens to me, and I try to stay positive that I am going to be okay. I know that one day my time on this earth will be over, but until then I plan to praise God for every day he gives me on this beautiful earth, and I plan to go as natural as possible with what I put in and on my body. That's really all I know that I can do. The rest is up to God.

CHAPTER TWO

Helping Myself

COMMITMENT

When I was real sick I survived with positive thinking that God was going to save me, and with the help of some spicy natural remedies to aid me with some of the inflammation symptoms and side effects that I was having. I had very little appetite, but I was swelling from inflammation. None of my clothes fit me right. Most of them were too little or too big for me, and when people stared at me, I would feel self-conscious about how I looked. No matter how healthy I tried to eat I just kept swelling up more and more. The more I learned about how some foods make more sugar in our bodies than others the more I realized that some of the so-called healthy food I was eating was killing me. To make things worse I had always been a soda and sweet tea junkie. I realized that things were getting scary, and that I had to be extreme with what I ate.

So, one day I said goodbye to the only two forbidden things that I allowed myself to have. I even cut down on sweet fruits because they made sugar in my body. The not so sweet fruits were okay, but my favorites were a thing of the past. After a couple of days without sugar and soda my stomach cramped, and I was extra nervous. I was having withdrawal from not having caffeine and sugar every day. Within a week or so I lost a little weight, but not enough. So, I done more research...

WHAT DID I FIND?

I found out that my uncle was right when he said to believe and think positive. I was positive that my grandmother's natural remedies would help me with the problems I was having. At the time all I had was food stamps to live off of. So, I done research for the types of food that could help with pain, anxiety, inflammation, and ways to shrink tumors. I remembered my grandmother telling me about old homemade remedies, like sassafras tea, and figured surely there had to be something online about what people use to use for illnesses before prescription medicines took over. I not only found out about foods that that could help with the symptoms I was having, that no one told me about, I also found ways to help with the blood clotting problem I was having, and with balance for the vertigo I had been suffering from because of the TIA's (transient ischemic attacks) caused by the blood clots.

I even found ways to lower my high blood pressure and triglycerides so that I did not have to take blood pressure or cholesterol medicine anymore. I was able to buy spices such as turmeric for pain and inflammation, garlic, raw honey and cinnamon to boost my immune system and fight off infections and viruses, and onions to help with my blood pressure. In the beginning I started off using too much of them and got sick. I done more research and started using them consistently at a moderate level. It was working. I also found out that by not only using certain foods and spices for inflammation and other symptoms I was having, I could also do a certain yoga exercise for vertigo with my ear down toward the floor to help my balance get better.

The more I learned the more hope I had at having a normal life. I started remembering my Uncle teaching me about positive thinking and being grateful for blessings in life, and I got the will to live again. I found that with spiritual awareness, some spicy natural remedies, and with a few balancing exercises that life was a lot sweeter than it had been before I started fighting harder for my life. It got a lot worse before it got better, but it did get better. As I started using the natural remedies my grandmother used to help others with, I realized that the things I never thought much about were suddenly all I had for hope. That and the grace of God.

MY MEDITATION METHOD

This is the method I use to meditate to help me focus on clearing my body of known illnesses. I also try to do this when I am down to help me focus on the good times in my life to help me stay positive and happy. I am sure that there things that may work better for other people, but this helps me stay focused on God and the blessings I have in this world.

WARNING!!!

Below you will find the method I used to meditate to help me believe and think positive. Please do not use my method without talking to your doctor first. Some food, spices, and exercises will interact with certain medications and diseases. What works for me may cause harm to you.

My Steps for Meditating

1. Look at medical pictures with the illness you have, and then look at medical pictures of what your body should look like without the cancer or illness. Sit or lay down in a quiet darkish room with a light shining in from another room. Close your eyes. Hear the sounds in the background. Relax and breath. Feel the air in your lungs.

2. Feel what you are sitting or lying on. Feel the air temperature

on your skin without touching your skin. Feel the temperature on your fingers. Feel how heavy you are and imagine yourself lighter. Imagine there is a happy feeling in the other room where the light is. Imagine that you are going closer to the light to find out what the happiness is about.

3. When you get to the light feel its warmth and think of a happy experience you had in the past. Using positive thinking, what did it feel like? Imagine the happiness you felt at the time. Feel it again. Let your happiness slowly move over every inch of your body until you fill the heaviness of where you sit or lay with the light feeling of happiness. Let your happiness spread to where the cold hard illness is, and let it cover the illness completely.

4. Let the warmth of the happiness soften the illness. Mentally see the illness shrink to a smaller size, and then imagine it exploding and vanishing into thin air. NOT IMAGINE IT FLOATING OFF OR IT MAY POSSIBLY SPREAD TO ANOTHER AREA!

5. See a mental picture of the area with no illness at all. See the empty spot where the cancer was, and see the area close in with healthy tissue, and see it as though it was normal. Believe that you are being healed. Give thanks for being healed. Tell yourself and believe that you are a survivor. You Win!

6. Feel the happiness of being cancer and illness free and having another chance at life. See yourself doing something fun. Feel the energy and excitement you have. Feel where you sit or lay. Feel your skin, fingers, and toes. Feel how alive they feel.

7. Breath in and feel the fresh air move through every area in your lungs. It feels so good to feel the air in your lungs. Hear the sounds in the background. Open your eyes slowly and see the colors around you. Be grateful that you can see what you see, feel, and hear what you see, feel, and hear. If you cannot see or hear then be grateful that you can feel.

8. Be grateful that you are alive and have a chance to witness to others to help them overcome what you have already survived. Feel the excitement of being blessed and knowing that you are

going to be okay. No matter what, it is okay. It is just temporary to prove, or learn, your strength. Tomorrow is another day. Smile.

9. This is one of the natural remedies that takes time and practice to perfect. No matter how I felt I did not give up. I done it every day. Afterwards, if I was able, I would listen to happy music or watch a clean comedy movie. Nothing sad. Love, happiness, and laughter heals my spirit, soul, body, and mind.

Tools Needed

1. A recording of your voice talking softly telling you what to do and think.

2. Soundtrack of natural beach sounds or some other relaxing sounds of nature.

3. Pictures of the different stages of the type of cancer, or illness, that you have.

4. Normal medical pictures of what the cancer area could look like without cancer.

MY FAVORITE REMEDIES

I realized that the things my grandmother talked about when I was growing up, were the very things I needed to help me with the symptoms I was having. I found out that just by taking away refined sugars and adding some simple spices and certain foods to my diet, that I could stop feeding the cancer with unnecessary sugar and hormones, and I could also turn some of the damage around. Below you will find the food, spices, and exercises that I use, why I use them, and how I used them when I was sicker.

WARNING!

Remember I am not a doctor. Please do not add food, spices, or exercises to your routine without talking to your doctor first. Please do not use my method without talking to your doctor first. Some food, spices, and exercises will interact with certain medications and diseases. What works for me may cause harm to you.

MY FAVORITE FOODS AND SPICES

These are my main sources of natural remedies that I use to help me keep inflammation in control. Please so not use them without talking to your Pharmasist and doctor first. Some foods and exercises interact with certain medical conditions and medicines.

Raw Clover Honey

One teaspoon to two tablespoons of Raw Clover Honey daily with Cinnamon is a good antioxidant that helps rid my body of impurities, fights inflammation, and helps me to fight cancer and other illnesses. If I am sick, I use the higher does by dividing it up into three doses. Morning, afternoon, evening.

Cinnamon

I use one teaspoon of Ceylon Cinnamon or one-half teaspoon of Cassia Cinnamon mixed into raw honey daily. Too much cinnamon a day causes liver damage. Something they don't tell us when we overload our self with cinnamon sweets when buying that cinnamon bread or cinnamon rolls and then we too many of them eat them every day.

Research tells me that it helps with my metabolism, is a good antioxidant and anti-inflammatory, helps lower high blood pressure by lowering bad cholesterol and triglycerides, increases good cholesterol, lowers blood sugar levels, helps fight Alzheimer's and Parkinson's disease, helps fight cancer by reducing cancer growth, fights bacteria and fungus, and is a good anti-viral remedy. I did not eat this when I felt constipated because it helps with diarrhea, so I did not want to make constipation worse.

Turmeric

One fourth to one half teaspoon two to three times daily of turmeric cooked lightly in my meals with a small amount of cayenne pepper in my vegetables and something fatty (such as fish or milk) works as a great anti-aging, anti-inflammatory, and antioxidant that helps with pain from arthritis, depression (works like Prozac), and Alzheimer's disease by boosting brain function. It helps blood pressure by reducing blood clots, and fights cancer by killing cancer cells and slowing tumor growth. I blend in garlic, parsley, onion, and very little cloves.

Ginger

Another natural remedies item on my "How to Survive Cancer" list is one half to one teaspoon of ginger once a day early in the morning is a strong anti-inflammatory and antioxidant that helps me survive cancer and fight cold and flu symptoms by reducing nausea and aids digestion. It is also used to help with arthritis and muscle soreness. It too boosts brain function and helps with Alzheimer's disease, helps to lower blood pressure, fights bacteria and cancer.

I mix it into my scrambled eggs or one-half cup oatmeal mixed with a little whole milk, one-half teaspoon dark chocolate, and one-fourth cup of mixed fruit. No sugar. I do not mix this with the cloves. Every time I tried it would cause me to get nauseous. I keep them at least two hours apart.

Garlic

Garlic is a big deal in my home. I use a lot of it, but only cook it lightly in my meals. Two to four cloves of fresh garlic daily when I am sick because it is high in manganese, vitamin C, and vitamin B6. Garlic boosts my immune system and helps to fights colds and viruses. It helps lower cholesterol and high blood pressure. It's also helps to fight Alzheimer's, Dementia, and other diseases. It helps with fatigue und detoxes my body, helps with menopause symptoms, inflammation, osteoarthritis, and bone density.

I found out the hard way not to mix garlic with yogurt or cloves. It truly messed my good bacteria up in my stomach, and it took me weeks to get over it. I should have done more research first. If I had I would have known to wait at least two hours before eating yogurt after having a lot of garlic, because garlic also has antifungal properties and the calcium in the yogurt prevents it from breaking down as it should.

Cloves

One thing on my "How to Survive Cancer" home remedies list is about one-eighth to one-fourth teaspoon of ground cloves no more than once a day to help fight off fungus, boosts brain function, and fight cancer by stopping the growth of tumors. It is an anti-bacteria spice that detoxes your liver. But eating it with calcium or eating too much of it can hurt your liver. It also helps with osteoporosis, help to control blood sugar by lowering it, and helps heal stomach ulcers by aiding with digestion to give your stomach a chance to heal on it's own.

Dark Chocolate

Dark chocolate is good to have on the natural remedies list. It is soothing and it relaxes me, and it is a good antioxidant that helps fight cancer and inflammation. It also helps me with positive thinking by putting me in a happy place. I buy the dark cocoa powder and use it for all my chocolate recipes.

Cherries and Blueberries

Dark tart cherries and fresh blueberries every day are good

antioxidants that fights inflammation. Dark cherries burst cancer cells so my immune system can fight off the disease. I would not recommend eating this if you have an aggressive cancer until after you have it under control unless your doctor says you can.

Pink Salmon and Tuna

Tuna or wild caught Pink Salmon a one to two times a week gives my body the healthy fat I need for my brain and to help with maintaining my cholesterol level.

Broccoli and Spinach

Broccoli and fresh spinach are two more to add to the natural remedies list as some of the how to survive cancer foods. They are good antioxidants that are naturally full of vitamin C, and it is said they fight cancer by slowing it down. Be careful if you have gout. Too much of any dark green vegetable, fish, or wheat will trigger gout symptoms. Also, they have Vitamin K that can interact with aspirin or blood thinners and keep them from working properly because Vitamin K helps to form blood clots.

Nuts

Just a hand full of Cashews, Pecans, Peanuts, or Walnuts every day give me healthy fat, fiber, and satisfy my snack cravings. They help to lower bad cholesterol and blood pressure. They are full of copper, iron, magnesium, and zinc. The magnesium helps with muscle cramps. Be careful though if you have anxiety issues. Just like potatoes, peanuts have caffeine in them. Too many peanuts can trigger anxiety.

Carrots

Carrots give me lots of fiber. They also have Vitamin A, Vitamin C, and beta-carotene. I think a lot of us have heard that they are good for our eyes. I believe that. I also know that when I eat them, they give me a small burst of energy. Some people say not to eat them because they are a night-root vegetable, but I believe the power they have must explode cells in our body and may work like cherries. They may burst cancer cells allowing my immune system to attack the cancer. I eat them fresh without salad dressing or heated on low with spices until they are tender.

Vidalia Onions

One or two one-fourth to one-half inch of sliced Vidalia Onion once to three times daily is good for reducing blood clots, high blood pressure, and cholesterol. It is known to helps with asthma, bronchitis, colds, cough, and different viruses. It helps with digestion and helps to cure ulcers. It is good for oral infections, tooth decay, and helps fight cancer. I eat it raw or cook it no more than five minutes over low to medium heat to save the healing powers it possesses. When my cholesterol was too high, I ate one whole small vidalia onion a day.

I did not eat one larger than that because I found that if I ate too much of this that I would get a large amount of dry skin on the bottom of my feet. When that happened, I would mix one teaspoon each of Vitamin D ointment, cocoa butter, and Vitamin E oil and applied it to my feet twice daily. Or I would use a skin tonic of two-thirds part grapeseed oil, one-third part coconut oil, with two added teaspoons of extra virgin olive oil, and I would massage it in my feet at bedtime. Within just one day my feet would look and feel better. After a couple of days, they would be healed.

Sauerkraut

Puts good bacteria in your stomach to help fight bad bacteria. I eat it as a side dish once to twice a week slightly warmed up and plain. I have something crunchy to eat with it and it seems to take away some of the tart pucker I get. Also, I learned that sauerkraut helps to keep me from having parasite problems.

Cayenne Pepper

One-eighth to one-fourth teaspoon Cayenne Pepper helps blood cells explode and allows your immune system to attack free radicals. Some say not to use pepper because your liver can't flush it. I don't know if they are referring to black pepper or cayenne pepper. Personally, I use Cayenne Pepper because I was told not to eat black pepper when I had kidney stones. Since I stopped using black pepper, I haven't had any more problems with kidney stones. I don't use very much of it because it is so hot and spicy.

Extra Virgin Olive Oil

One teaspoon to two tablespoons of Cold Pressed Extra Virgin Olive Oil is a good Omega 3 for your cholesterol. I use it uncooked on my vegetables, and I also cook my scrambled eggs in it on low heat so as not to cause it to break down. The downside to it is that it is high in calories, so be mindful of how much you use.

Parsley

Eating parsley every day helps to get rid of bad breath and body odor caused from eating a lot of fish and garlic.

Ground Flaxseed

One to two tablespoons of ground Flaxseed is a good Omega 3 to fight cholesterol, and it is a good antioxidant. It makes a natural estrogen hormone, so cancer patients who have hormone related cancer need to be careful not to use too much. Or not at all may be best. I love it because it can be used as an egg replacement in recipes to help hold them together, and it makes your hair shiny. It can even restore your natural hair color if you have early grey hair due to a vitamin deficiency.

Fresh Turkey

Eating plain turkey without bread about thirty minutes to an hour before going to bed helps me rest better because it naturally makes L-tryptophan, niacin a B-vitamin, serotonin, and melatonin to help you relax and feel better. Some say that it doesn't work. If that is true, then the power of belief kicks in because it works for me. It is also supposed to help with anxiety too.

Raw Unfiltered Apple Cider Vinegar

One teaspoon to two tablespoons of Raw Unfiltered Apple Cider

Vinegar helps to fight infection, lower cholesterol, help with blood clots, and cleanse your body of toxins. Be careful. Don't use this without talking to your doctor first. best has pectin in it and may interact with certain medications.

Vanilla

Vanilla, and a few other fragrances, are good natural remedies to survive cancer because they relax me and give me a since of wellbeing. I do not use vanilla extracts, or any other extracts, because of the additives in them. If needed I use about one-fourth to one-half teaspoon of molasses for recipes to give them an added flavor.

MY FAVORITE EXERCISES

I force myself to exercise even when I don't feel well. Doctors insisted that I exercise. Not only does exercising regularly give me more energy, it helps to keep blood clots building up causing me to have a stroke. So, I force myself to exercise unless I am extremely ill.

Besides dancing my favorite exercises are ...

Stretching

I start off by sitting straight up in a chair, and then extend my legs out one at a time. When doing so I stretch my legs while flexing my feet and toes. One at a time I raise my arms up over my shoulder behind my head while placing the other arm behind my back and stretch them towards each other. The goal is to overlap my fingers, but because one of my arms is disfigured, they cannot touch. They don't even come close to it. But I try anyway.

Then I do stretches on the floor. I lay flat on my back and stretch my hands over my head as far as I can while stretching my legs and toes out as far as they will go. I raise one leg up in the air and cross it over to the other side while flexing my toes. I repeat with the other leg. I lay on my back and raise both my legs up in the air. I spread them out as far as I can, and then bend them in to touch the heels of my feet together. I gently press down on my thighs to put pressure on them. I put my legs back down and stretch them out again. Then I bend my knees and put my heels flat on the floor and spread my legs apart as far as I can and tilt my hip up and down several times. I roll over on to my stomach and stretch out as far as I can.

I bend one leg up bringing my heel as close to my buttock that I can. Then I pull it towards me with my hand on the same side. I relax it and repeat with the other side. Then I stretch out as far as I can again. After that I set up and cross one leg in front of me and stretch out to touch my toes on the other leg. I repeat it with the other side. I then put one leg over the other one, and while holding the upper leg in place I slowly twist my upper body the opposite direction. Then I do the other side. Then I lean over in front of me as far as I can and move back and forth from left to right, and then back to the left, and then back to the middle. I then use the strap I got while in physical therapy to put around my feet and pull towards me while resisting with my foot.

I end my floor exercises with balancing stretches by stretching out as far as I can while standing up straight and reaching out as far as I can with one arm at a time. I then raise my arms straight up over my head and with my feet together I bend my knees. Then I raise one leg up bended and straighten it out. I hold it there as long as I can. Then I repeat it using the other side. I stretch my arms out again, and then stretch my neck slightly in different directions so as not to cause too much pressure on it. Then I relax and drink a glass of water.

Exercise Springs

I use my exercise spring to strengthen my stomach, legs and back. While standing, I place my feet in the feet holders, bend my knees, and while holding the handles I pull straight up and hold my position as long as I can. Then I repeat it several times. Then I shake it out.

Mini Stair Stepper

I use my mini stair stepper not only to strengthen my thighs and build muscle, but also to help with my balance. While using my mini stair stepper I stretch my arms up over my head and then hold them out to my side while stepping. I also stand straight up on it and do squats with my arms out in front of me and to my side. I do steps and stretches to music to help me keep a rhythm.

Exercise Ball

I totally love my exercise ball, and I use it all the time. I use it for doing pushups, and for sitting on it and trying to balance myself while holding my arms out to the side and raising my feet up off the floor. I can't help but to giggle when I go rolling a little. Sometimes it gets scary when I lose my balance and go flying off towards something. When that happens, I put my feet back on the ground.

I also use my exercise ball as a foot stool to hold my feet up while sitting down watching television or working on my laptop. It allows me to move my feet around and lightly exercise them by bending my knees while rolling it towards and away from me with my calves and feet, and even pulling my feet up close to me and putting my heels together on it. Besides walking, I think it is my main source of exercise.

Yoga Balancing Exercises

Learning how to use some balancing exercises helps me with my balance, gives me more energy, and helps me to feel more confident about my movements. It is also good with connecting to my inner self so that I can vision the cancer breaking apart and melting away, and it helps to balance my system at the core.

Vertigo Exercises

When my eyes start to float or flutter, I know it is time to do my vertigo exercises, even before I start to experience vertigo. It helps to lessen the symptoms, and sometimes prevent it from happening. I lay on the bed on my back and let my head hang off the end. Then I turn on my head left and let my head hang down, then roll my head back again, then I do my right side, and back over on my back.

I then roll over on my stomach and let my head hang down from that angle. I do this for about 10 minutes. If I feel a little unsteady, I get down on the floor on my knees and put my forehead on the floor, then roll my head over while keeping in contact with the floor and put my right ear as flat on the floor as I can. I roll to the center and on over to my left ear. Then back to my forehead.

I stretch my body out straight with my chin on the floor, and then slowly raise myself up off the floor. Usually this works for me, but don't do it without talking to your doctor.

Music and Dancing

I love to listen to music. I believe it should always be included on a how to survive cancer list. Music sooths my nerves, and then it excites me and helps me to stay in a positive thinking mode. I can't help tapping to the beat. I love to exercise my lungs with singing. I'm not sure what my family or the neighbors think about it. I know I can't sing good, but no one has complained yet. I get short of breath, but I push myself as far as I can, afterwards I am able to cough up some of the stuff down in my lungs. So, I try to exercise my lungs as often as possible. I would much rather sing than to blow hard in a stubborn incentive spirometer. However, I must admit, those help too.

Balancing in Water

Whenever I have the opportunity, I like to do balancing exercises in the swimming pool. After doing some stretches, I like to use a foam tube in the pool to lean on evenly with my arms. I slowly raise my legs up off the swimming pool floor and bring them straight in front of me as if I was sitting with my legs out straight.

I hold it for about ten seconds, then I slowly lower them and without touching the bottom I keep my knees bent, I push the foam tube straight down with both hands to keep my balance and to help me pull my legs behind me and slowly straighten them out while slowly raising the foam tube back up to the surface of the water.

I float with my back side facing upwards while holding my head up out of the water with my arms crossed laying on top of the foam tube while holding the foam tube firmly so as not to lose my grip or balance. I hold it for as long as I can. I also like to lean backwards on the tube holding on to it with it lined up behind my shoulders. I put my arms over it and swim with backwards strokes.

Have you heard of the fish that swims backwards? I like to swim backwards too, but it's hard for me to do. While holding on to the foam tube I balance myself, and with my feet raised up off the pool bottom I make my legs and feet do running motions as if I was pedaling a bicycle. I make sure to keep my toes at a down angle to push the water away from me to go forward. I do this from one side of the pool to the other side.

Then before I touch the other side, I switch the direction my feet are going as if I was pedaling backwards. I make sure to keep my toes angled upwards to pull the water towards me. It's hard, but after a few seconds I start to go backwards, and I adjust the tube holding on to it firmly with my forearms laying on it to keep my balance. I do it all the way back to the other side of the pool.

After thirty minutes of doing different exercises in the pool I get out on the low end of the pool using the steps. As I approach the low end, I swish each leg back and forth several times. As I approach the steps I stop right before the bottom step and shake my legs back and forth several times each. As I approach the next step, I stop half-way up and do the same thing. I stop on the next step and do the same thing. I shake each leg back and forth between each step and while standing on the next step. I do this all the way out, and then do it from the pool side while holding on to the handrail.

If I have to use the ladder to get out with, I do the same thing while sitting backwards on the steps making sure not to lose my grip on the ladder. This keeps me from having a heavy feeling in my legs, or from feeling dizzy and off balance by helping the blood get from my lower legs back up to my heart.

CHAPTER THREE

My "I Believe" Faith Kept Me Alive

I BELIEVE

Because of my uncle teaching me about God's power I held on to my belief that thoughts and words have power in our lives even when it felt like I was dying. I was, and I still am, thankful for every day I can be on this beautiful earth. I love life, and people, and I know that I am lucky to be alive. I have survived some truly horrible things in life, and I have had to watch others suffer, and sometimes die, and I still hold on to my faith that words have power. If we truly belief without a doubt that something will happen (not just can happen) then it is truly possible it will happen. You have to be thankful for it before receiving it and go on with your life like it is no longer an issue and is resolved. Take care of whatever needs to be taken care of but do so with the idea that it's just something that has to be done and it's no big deal. Some say that is delusional. Well, maybe to a point it does seem delusional. But not in a since that we cannot accept or recognize reality. It is just putting faith in our higher power who holds the key to all creation and realizing that anything is possible through our creator. It has worked for me, and it has worked for many others. So, surely there must be something to it.

I also believe that God gave us the power to help ourselves with some of the natural resources that we have been given on this beautiful planet. In my research to understand more about natural home remedies I came to realize that most of the natural resources that are known of are in areas where they are needed the most or where an illness originated from.   God knew people would have some sort of issue with certain illnesses or contact with certain plants in those areas and created antidotes for most of those issues. There may be antidotes for all of them and we just don't know what they are yet. I think there is no other way of describing that other than divine intervention. No one on earth could ever convince me that it was just random explosions of existence that created them. I was told by someone who majored in science in college that the reason the antidotes are found in the region of where illnesses originated in is because it was the antidote plant that caused the illness to begin with. The antidote is just like a flu vaccine. That may be partially true, but in my opinion, it is still too structured to be an accident. We have a creator. How did our creator come to exist? I don't know. I do not question it anymore like I used to, because no one but the creator would know. I am just grateful that the creator created me just like I believe our creator created you and those natural resources we need to survive, or to aid in some of the symptoms from illnesses we may have to endure.

Those natural resources are where a lot of medications we use origin from. Doctors and scientist research and use those resources to aid us in our treatment of those illnesses. Most of us do not have the education to know about the resources we could use to help ourselves. Rather it be from professional education or from life teachings passed down through family generations as it was with my family. As time has passed most traditional teachings have disappeared because we have turned to technology for our knowledge. Technology is only as smart as what those who have programmed it to be. People only put what they thought was most important in those programs to save data space or time. They left out a lot of things that had been passed down through generations by our ancestors that were used for daily survival that could help us have a better quality of life. Things like natural remedies that can help us become survivors from diseases that would normally kill us if our immune system got too weak to fight it off.

I was fortunate enough to have had elderly family members who still practiced using some of those old home remedies, and who taught me the importance of using them. I am concerned for our future generations because without the knowledge of these natural remedies that have been passed down from past generations these natural remedy aids could be lost forever. That would leave people at the mercy of pharmaceutical companies for everything they need to fight off illness. When I was younger, I knew and used a lot of the teachings that my grandparents passed down to me to help myself and my children. I want them to know what I know so that they can pass it down to their children. That is the only way that I know of to keep the medical industry that run medical facilities like assembly factories pushing dangerous drugs on us because we have no other options and thus taking complete control of our health care.

I am not saying that all medicines are bad for you, or that all doctors and medical facilities are cold hearted and in it just for the money and power. I am only saying that even though they are greatly needed we might want to look at trying to help ourselves before handing our life over to others to decide if we should live or die. Those doctors get paid, or get discounts, for pushing those new medicines on us. Even though it is with good intentions on the doctor's part, the companies that make the stuff are not always truthful with us, or they downplay the dangers of the medicines. So, in my opinion I believe that those medicines should be the last thing to try when traditional remedies are not strong enough for what a person is suffering with. Think about it. If the medical condition is able to be solved with a surgery, but you choose to take dangerous medicine instead of having the surgery, and then you get bad side effects from those medicines that need other medicines to help you with those side effects, and that medicine causes different side effects that needs medicine to help with it then who is the one profiting from you taking the medicine? You or the companies that made the medicine?

Dying from cancer complications is not dying from cancer. It is dying from the medicine you took to keep the cancer from killing you. Unless you have an aggressive cancer, you may be better off without all those chemicals in your body. Up the dose of some natural foods to boost your immune system so that your miracle working body can have a chance to cure itself before you fill it full of toxins that will shorten your life anyway. In my opinion, and my belief, people who push medicine that they know will kill us or cause shorter life spans are people working toward downsizing the world's overpopulation problem and using the survival of the fittest methods to do it. They are taking advantage of it and getting rich off of the sick and insurance companies that are paying for the sick and poor to be weeded out.

Not many years ago natural resources were easy to find and use. Now days you have to dig hard to find the research on those natural remedies that have almost disapeared, and when you can find the resources even the natural foods are contaminated with farm chemicals because of it being in the ground, air, and water. The only reason why I am saying these things is because I feel times are getting worse and our country is taking a major step backwards, and I believe that it is time to fight the real problem. Being separated. The groups who are trying to keep people separated so no one is paying attention to them will continue to do so until the average person is not able survive without them. All real knowledge about natural resources, religion, art, history, native languages, and giving equal treatment will all be gone from us for good. Only the rich, strong, and needed will be able to survive unless people learn how to use natural resources to survive like they have had to do for centuries. Until now.

MORE ABOUT THE AUTHOR

I BELIEVE IN GOD'S NATURAL REMEDIES, AND I CARE.

Like I said before I am a breast cancer survivor and the mother of four, one in Heaven, and I have eleven grandchildren. I am also one of those country city girls who loves life and believes in the power of healing. I have a bit of a southern accent that you will either love or think something is wrong with me. Either way I surprised a lot of doctors for living way past the six months to a year and a half life expectancy that they said I had. Not once, but several times.

I believe that I owe my healing to God, the help of some good doctors, and some natural resources that God put on this beautiful earth to give us relief from some of the bad things that may come with just being alive. Things such as cancer, fungus from exposure to mold, high blood pressure from lack of exercise and eating things that are bad for us, and diabetes passed down from our family genes. I lost my grandmother, and my mother-in-law to cancer.

I don't know why they did not make it any longer than they

did, but I am grateful for each new day that God allows me the privilege to love and enjoy this beautiful world that we live in. Raising my children alone, and going through cancer, sometimes left me feeling as if I was in a haze. Out of weakness from being tired of doing it all alone I believe that I became venerable and fell as prey for a couple of predators.

During that time, I went through confusion that I could not explain. Thank God, I was able to pull myself together, and move on with my life. During that time, I kept records of my confused feelings. I finally woke up, buried my shame, and sought outside help. I realized that what other people done to me was not my problem. My problem was how I was going to let it affect me. My biggest problem was learning how recognize anxiety and stop it before it started.

I want to help others. I want others who are suffering pain, vertigo, nausea, fatigue, anxiety, and depression from any illness, or from side effects from prescription medications, to know that I care about what you or someone you care about are going through. I want to share my journey about some of the struggles I went through from not being able to support myself because of my illness being so bad, and the simple things I done that help me have a better quality of life.

I think the hardest part was learning how to relearn how to learn, and how to be consistent while I used my body as a human guinea pig to test my research on natural remedies. Though I still am not healed, I have a better life than what I had before I discovered the power inside of me and spicy natural remedies. Please understand that I am not a doctor or nutritionist.

I am just a breast cancer survivor who has done a lot of research on home remedies, and who has used some of the things I learned while fighting for my life to live a more normal life. I recommend that if you decide to try using any home remedies, or new exercises, that you talk with your doctor and pharmacist first. Some food and spices can interact with certain medications and diseases. What works for me may not work for you, and it may harm you.

WHAT ELSE DO I BELIEVE

I believe in the power of positive thinking

Small things mean a lot to me. I believe that we have a higher power, I believe that we are all born equal and have a life source that is affected by what we believe and who we associate with. Negative attracts negative, and positive attracts positive. I believe that once you fall into the negative zone it is hard to get out of. And that it takes a conscious effort to change your subconscious that retains information without you even trying to.

I believe in focusing on the colors to help distract away from what is negative. Besides learning about natural remedies I like watching comedy movies, singing, listening to just about any kind of music besides head banging, cursing, and music that leaves you feeling sad. I like listening to old phonographs of radio talk shows, almost all kinds of art including stage plays and concerts. I like collecting old pictures, playing Parchisi and Yahtzee, making a personal websites, writing short stories and poetry.

I also like BBQ, cooking from scratch. I also like going out to eat, but have allergies, so my options of restaurant foods are limited. I like fishing, camping and cooking over the open fire, sports including football, hockey, ice skating, roller derby, the Olympics, baseball, gymnastics, tennis, dancing, golf, and too many other things to mention. However, I'm not a fanatic. I only like to watch them. I'm not super woman so I don't play them, anymore. I like going to the park and swinging on the swings, going to the zoo, traveling the world through the internet, monster truck shows, car shows, going to flea markets and yard sales to see what treasures are waiting to be found. Hopefully one day I will find my jewelry box. I like going to the ocean, watching the sun set and rise, discovering new things about nature rather it be in a book, on the internet, documentaries on television, in a museum, the zoo, or on a small hike.

I forgot a lot of things I knew, and rather I am relearning, or finding out for the first time, I am amazed at how everything is organized and linked together. I think this world is awesome. Sure, there are a lot of haters in it, but I can't let them make me miss out on the wonder of being alive just because they choose to hate. All I can do is pray for them to have a caring conscious mind so that their hearts will open to how we are all linked together. I like to travel with my feet near the ground. I had my share of air travel when I was younger. A few places I would like to go to are the Grand Canyon, Yosemite Park, Las Vegas, Houston to visit a certain church, and New York. I spent my vacation with a friend in Springfield Massachusetts when my children were all less than four years old. We boarded a train in Orlando Florida and then transferred to a sleeper coach in Tallahassee, and then spent the next three days traveling on trains.

Trying to get from one car to another over those flaps in the middle alone with three small children was something I wasn't prepared for. Thankfully there were good people who helped me with them. That weekend we drove down to New York New York and got lost in the Bronx trying to find the Statue of Liberty. I heard it can be rough there, but the men who gave us directions to get back on the right road gave us good directions, so there is a lot to be said about the good that is there too. Two weeks later we took the train back to Orlando, but that time I was more prepared with plenty of food and supplies, so we didn't have to make that trip to the diner car. I would not of missed the trip for the world, but I swore that I would never do it again. However, if given the chance to go back I would, and I would like to take in a few shows and see the Statue of Liberty up close. I can just imagine how awesome it would be. I truly love big city lights, and I would love to see New York at night.

I also love God, praying for people, and doing volunteer work, this should have been the first thing on the list. I don't drink or smoke, but I did smoke a little when I was younger, and I am active with my family. Such as babysitting and going to school events. I am looking forward to the day I can see them all graduate.

Thank you for your time and support.

May the light in you always shine.

RESOURCES

U. S. National Library of Medicine
https://www.nlm.nih.gov/

All natural remedies listed in this book can be cross referenced through the U. S. National Library of Medicine.

Made in the USA
Monee, IL
07 July 2026

56550104R00079